THE BOOK
OF
LOSERS

THE BOOK OF LOSERS

An Irresistible Litany of Failure
Through the Ages

George Rooks

ST. MARTIN'S PRESS • New York

Copyright © 1980 by George Rooks

All rights reserved. For information, write:
St. Martin's Press, Inc., 175 Fifth Ave., New York, N.Y. 10010.

Manufactured in the United States of America

Library of Congress Cataloging in Publication Data

Rooks, George.
  The book of losers.

I.   Losers.   I.   Title.
AG243.R58   031'.02   80-14681
ISBN 0-312-08956-2

DESIGN BY DENNIS J. GRASTORF

To:

Oakland, cheap wine, dirt bikes, sushi, psychiatrists, English departments, prime-time TV, "mellow," mosquitoes, Spanish trains, Road Runner, and bad breath (for obvious reasons)
and
to my best friends, Linda and George, who never lost the faith!

Contents

I	Losers of Body Functions, Parts, and Conditions	1
II	Losers of Life	37
III	Political Losers	68
IV	Military Losers	85
V	Money Losers	99
VI	Movie Star Losers	119
VII	Sports Losers	126

THE BOOK
OF
LOSERS

–1–

Losers of Body Functions, Parts, and Conditions

PEOPLE WHO LOST THEIR HEADS

> *If you can keep your head when all about you*
> *Are losing theirs . . .*
> *Yours is the Earth and everything that's in it,*
> *And—which is more—you'll be a Man, my son!*
> RUDYARD KIPLING, "If"

1. John the Baptist, Hebrew prophet (1st century B.C.)

Angered by the Baptist's denunciation of her incestuous marriage to Herod (her brother-in-law), Herodias sought revenge by asking her daughter Salome to surprise Herod with a birthday dance. Salome so pleased her stepfather that he promised her anything she wished. Spurred on by her mother, Salome requested John's head: "And the king was sorry: nevertheless for the oath's sake, and them which sat with him at meat, he commanded it to be given her. And he sent, and beheaded John

1

2 THE BOOK OF LOSERS

in the prison. And his head was brought in a charger, and given to the damsel: and she brought it to her mother." (Matthew 14:9–11)

2. St. Paul, Roman Apostle of Jesus (1st century A.D.)

For many years Paul eluded execution because of his special status as a Roman citizen. However, Nero reached the point at which he could no longer abide Paul's message of Christianity. One day while the Apostle was preaching, Nero ordered his soldiers to arrest him. They then took him to a place of execution outside the city, where he lost his head by the sword.[1]

3. St. Alban, British religious leader (?–287)

Originally a pagan, Alban was converted to Christianity by his friend Amphibalus. When the governor of the province sent his soldiers to arrest Amphibalus, Alban disguised himself as his friend so that Amphibalus could escape. When the trick was discovered, the governor sentenced Alban to be scourged and beheaded. According to the religious historian Bede, Alban's executioner underwent a religious conversion and asked permission to die with him. Permission was readily granted, and a nearby soldier beheaded them both on June 22.[1]

4. St. George, patron saint of England (?–303)

George was serving in Diocletian's army during the Christian persecutions, when he suddenly quit his command. He then went brazenly to the senate house at Nicomedia, proclaimed his Christianity, and ridiculed the paganism of the senators. After the senators recovered from their astonishment, they ordered local authorities to torture George, drag him through the streets, and behead him the following day; the sentence was executed as prescribed.[1]

LOSERS OF BODY FUNCTIONS 3

5. Anne Boleyn, Queen of England (1504–1536)

Upon being condemned to death, Anne asked that her decapitation not be performed by a common headsman with an axe, but by an experienced swordsman; in deference to her wishes, such a man was procured from Calais. On the straw-covered scaffold (so covered to soak up her blood), she prayed while an attendant blindfolded her, and she prostrated herself before the block: "O God, have pity on my soul; O God, have pity on my soul; O God have pity————." At this point the blade of the sword severed her neck, and "her little head rolled into the straw." At once, her lifeless trunk was lifted (blood still flowing) into a coffin, and taken to be buried.[2]

6. Lady Jane Grey, Queen of England (1537–1554)

On the morning of their execution, Jane refused to see her husband despite his pleas, believing that it would only make the ordeal more difficult for each of them. From her window at the Tower, she watched as he was led to the scaffold, and could see his headless body as it was carted away. With no tears, she prayed quietly as she was taken to the scaffold. Upon reaching it, she sprang up the steps, let down her hair and uncovered her neck. Then she granted the hangman forgiveness, and knelt down saying: "I pray you dispatch me quickly; will you take it off before I lay me down?" Assured that he would not, the blindfolded Jane was guided to the block—where she stretched forth her body, and said: "Lord into thy hands I commend my spirit." With those words, the axe fell.[2]

7. Mary, Queen of Scots (1542–1587)

After a short prayer on the scaffold, she placed her head on the block. However, she mistakenly put her hands under her neck, and the executioners had to gently remove them so that they

4   THE BOOK OF LOSERS

would not interfere with the blow of the axe. Then as one executioner held her slightly, the other struck the blow. Unfortunately, even though he was a professional headsman, the act of beheading a queen had unnerved him, and the axe hit the knot of the handkerchief binding her eyes. The blow scarcely cut the skin. Mary neither moved nor spoke, and at the second stroke her head fell from her shoulders.[2]

8. Robert Devereux, Earl of Essex (1566–1601)

The earl came dressed for the occasion in a black cloak with a black doublet, and a scarlet waistcoat with long scarlet sleeves. After a long prayer, which included best wishes for the queen's welfare, he removed his outer clothing and put his head on the block. Crying out: "Lord, into thy hands I commend my spirit!" he lay flat on the scaffold and stretched out his hands—and the axe fell. However, it took three strokes to completely chop off the earl's head, which the executioner then lifted by its hair to show to the crowd with the words: "God save the Queen!"[2]

9. Sir Walter Raleigh, English courtier, navigator, author (1552–1618)

On the morning of his execution, Raleigh took communion, ate breakfast, and smoked his pipe as usual. According to those around him, he even seemed excited by the scene which was before him. At 8:00 A.M. he was taken to the scaffold, and joked with one of his friends who was trying to get a better view: "I know not what shift you will make, but I am sure to have a place." After mounting the scaffold, he asked the executioner to let him see the axe; upon running his finger down the edge, he remarked: "This is sharp medicine, but it is a sound cure for all diseases." Then he knelt down and placed his head on the block. After a short prayer he gave the signal; the headsman severed his head with only two blows.[2]

LOSERS OF BODY FUNCTIONS

10. Charles I, King of England (1600–1649)

When taken to the scaffold, he was initially concerned that the block was too low for the axeman to get the proper leverage. After being told that securing another block was impossible, he took off his cloak and said: "Remember." Then he put on the white cap to keep his hair from his neck, and refused to give the executioner the customary pardon, saying only: "I pray you, do not put me to pain." His final words were: "I shall say but a short prayer and, when I hold my hands thus, strike." When he gave the signal, his head was chopped off with a single blow. Once the king was dead, the scaffold became a marketplace, with the soldiers allowing members of the crowd to buy pieces of his hair, and to dip their handkerchiefs in his blood for a small charge.[2]

11. James, Duke of Monmouth, bastard son of English King Charles II (1649–1685)

The duke went to the place of execution with calm resolution. When he saw the axe, he asked to touch it, and remarked that it was not sharp enough. He gave the executioner half of the monetary present he intended, telling him that the other half would be given to him if he did his job well. He then lay flat on the scaffold, and the trembling headsman struck at his neck two or three times, but did not sever his head from the body. He threw the axe down, but the sheriff made him pick it back up. He took another three or four strokes before he was able to chop off the duke's head. Shortly afterward, the head was sewn back on the body so a formal painting could be made.[2]

12. Louis XVI, French emperor (1754–1793)

Arriving at the place of execution, Louis removed his hat, coat, and jacket, then untied his neck cloth and opened his shirt. The guards then seized him, tying his arms and cutting his hair to leave the neck exposed. He then climbed the scaffold, and said

6 THE BOOK OF LOSERS

in a loud voice: "I die innocent of all crimes laid to my charge; I pardon those who have occasioned my death; and I pray to God that the blood you are now going to shed may never be visited on France, and you, unfortunate people." The time was 10:20 A.M. when the guards seized Louis again, tied him to the upright plank, and fixed the heavy wooden collar around his neck. Unfortunately, because Louis's neck was so fat, the blade penetrated slowly , and a scream was heard before the head was completely severed. One of the executioners then picked it up and showed the head to the crowd, while making "atrocious and indecent" gestures.[3]

13. Marie Antoinette, Queen of France (1755–1793)

The queen had to be helped out of the cart that brought her to the scaffold, but in "her pretty plum shoes" climbed the ladder without assistance. On the way up, she stepped (apparently by mistake) on the executioner's foot, causing him to cry out in pain. She then turned around and remarked: "Monsieur, I beg your pardon. I did not do it on purpose." Once on the platform, she began to tremble from exhaustion until the executioner grabbed her and tied her to the plank. Four minutes later she was dead.[3]

14. Georges Danton, French politician (1759–1794)

At the foot of the scaffold, Danton exclaimed, "O my wife, my well-beloved wife, I shall never see thee more, then . . ." Regaining his composure, he calmed himself with: "Danton, no weakness!" He then remarked to a friend who stepped forward to meet him: "Our heads will meet *there*"—pointing to the headsman's sack. His last words were to the executioner: "Thou wilt show my head to the people; it is worth showing."[4]

LOSERS OF BODY FUNCTIONS 7

15. Maximilian Robespierre, French revolutionary (1758–1794)

When the cart carrying the prisoners reached the scaffold, the executioners took Robespierre out and laid him on the ground to wait his turn. Twenty-first out of twenty-two to be executed, he kept his eyes shut until he felt himself being carried up the blood-soaked platform. The crowd hushed as he stepped toward the plank, and he "heaved a sigh of pain" when he saw the guillotine. After having thrown down his coat, which was crossed over his shoulders, the executioner roughly tore away the bandage which was holding his bullet-riddled jaw together—causing the blood to gush out. Robespierre's scream of pain "like that of a slaughtered animal" reverberated from one end of the square to the other. A moment later the guillotine had done its work, and the executioner took the distorted head by the hair to display it to the people.[5]

16. Prince Faisal Ibn Musaed, Saudi-Arabia (1948–1975)

Faisal, who was educated at the universities of Colorado and California-Berkeley, was publicly beheaded in Riyadh, Saudi-Arabia, on June 18 for the assassination of his uncle King Faisal. Since a medical panel declared him sane, the death penalty was automatic under Islamic law. Faisal was led from his cell to Dira Square, where a court official read the verdict. His hands were tied behind his back, but he was not blindfolded, and appeared calm. As he knelt at the block, a security man poked him in the ribs with a stick to make his head jerk upward. At the same moment, the executioner beheaded him with one blow of his gold-handled sword. The prince's head was then put on a wooden stake and displayed to the applauding multitude, who chanted "Allah is great" and "Justice is done."[6]

THE BOOK OF LOSERS

SOURCES:
1. William Forbush, ed., *Fox's Book of Martyrs*. New York: Holt, Rinehart and Winston, 1962.
2. Leonard Parry, *The History of Torture in England*. Montclair, N.J.: Patterson Smith, 1975.
3. Vincent Cronin, *Louis & Antoinette*. New York: William Morrow, 1975.
4. Thomas Carlyle, *The French Revolution: A History*. New York: Heritage Press, 1956.
5. Stanley Loomis, *Paris in the Terror*. New York: J.B. Lippincott, 1964.
6. *Washington Post*, June 19, 1975.

PEOPLE WHO LOST THEIR MINDS

Can it be that they are mad themselves, since they call me mad?
PLAUTUS, *Menoechmi*

1. Saul, first King of Israel (11th century B.C.)

Early on, Saul exhibited psychopathic tendencies such as falling into ecstasies and prophesying future events. His condition worsened after he assumed the throne. Events took a decided turn for the worse when he believed that God had rejected him; he became abnormally suspicious, and could find relief only in the therapeutic strains of David's harp. Of course, he finally turned on David too, and attempted to kill him. Upon failing, he stripped naked, tore his hair, and wallowed on the floor for several days. He even tried killing his son Jonathan, but could only succeed in killing himself in battle with the Philistines.[1]

2. Caligula, Roman Emperor (A.D. 12–41)

When Caligula first became emperor he seemed relatively normal, but he soon succumbed to a debilitating madness. To

LOSERS OF BODY FUNCTIONS   9

begin with, he had most of his relatives (except Claudius and his sisters) murdered, usually amusing himself with their torture and execution while he dined. Indeed, he had such a voracious appetite for execution that he often expressed the wish that the entire Roman population had only one neck, so that he could kill them all with one stroke. His love life was mainly focused on his sister Drusilla (he sold his other sisters into prostitution), with whom he committed incest and whom he made a god—as he did himself. Not content to lavish his favors on Drusilla, Caligula also made his favorite horse a consul and a member of the college of priests. When his caprices became too much, he was assassinated by the Praetorian Guard.[2]

3. St. Francis of Assisi, founder of the Franciscan Order (1181–1226)

At the age of twenty-four, Francis was struck with a severe illness which kept him bedridden for several months. When he was able to move about again, he experienced a deep depression, and retreated to a nearby cave to find solace. Then one day he claimed he saw the image of the crucified Christ before him, but the sight depressed him even more. He began to wander around in his neighbors' fields with his face covered with tears. Finally, much to the embarrassment of his father, who tried to have him imprisoned, Francis started wearing beggar's clothes. This act of poverty was all the scandalized community could take; Francis's family and neighbors drove him out of town with stones. Nonetheless, his visionary zeal was contagious, and Pope Gregory IX canonized him in 1228.[3]

4. Jonathan Swift, English satirist (1667–1745)

For years Swift's sanity has been debated by academicians. Certainly, he often expressed the fear that he would die insane. Perhaps this fear was prompted by the fact that he spent a year of

10   THE BOOK OF LOSERS

his life without reading, speaking, or apparently recognizing anyone. Other bases for this fear might have been his rather unusual habit of walking ten hours a day, eating his meals standing, and viciously attacking people who entered his room unannounced. When Swift died in 1745, he left almost £11,000 to a lunatic asylum. An autopsy revealed "signs of enlarged and diseased arteries, and an extremely small cerebellum."[3]

5. Jean-Jacques Rousseau, Swiss author and philosopher (1712–1778)

Always despondent, Rousseau became paranoid in his later years. Once, in London, he became obsessed with the notion that he was about to be arrested. He quickly abandoned his luggage and money at his hotel, and made his harried way to France, selling portions of silver spoons. Upon arriving in France he begged to be put in the Bastille, but was turned down. Unable to trust anyone (he even thought his dog had an ulterior motive in licking him), he wrote a letter to God which he attempted to place on the altar at Notre Dame. However, he found the railing locked, and immediately suspected that God was also plotting against him. His only means of deriving peace was to have a woman beat him while he was naked. This and other tendencies led Voltaire to conclude that he was mad.[3]

6. Arthur Schopenhauer, German philosopher (1788–1860)

Convinced that the devil created the world, and prone to fits of extraordinary melancholy, Schopenhauer believed that evil spirits possessed him. He habitually roamed the streets of cities gesturing and talking loudly to himself, and acted with similar abandon at restaurants. Like Rousseau, he grew paranoid, moving from Naples for fear of smallpox, from Berlin for fear of cholera, from Verona for fear of someone poisoning his snuff. He refused to cut his beard, but insisted on burning the ends of

LOSERS OF BODY FUNCTIONS 11

it. Perhaps for this reason, he would only live on the first floor of buildings for fear of fire. Fearful of disease, he would never touch a glass that was not his own, and he wrote most of his business documents in Sanskrit, Greek, or Latin because he feared popular curiosity. Unlike Rousseau, Schopenhauer did trust his dog, and left most of his property to him when he died.[3]

7. Robert Schumann, German composer (1810–1856)

Schumann plunged into depression for no apparent reason when he was in his early twenties. By the time he was forty, he lived in constant terror of being sent to an insane asylum. The most visible evidence of his madness was his insistence that Beethoven and Mendelssohn dictated his musical scores to him from their tombs. In 1854 Schumann attempted suicide by jumping in the Rhine; however, he was saved and his worst fears were realized. The composer spent his last two years in a Bonn asylum; an autopsy revealed "thickening of the cranial membranes and atrophy of the brain."[3]

8. Charles Baudelaire, French poet (1821–1867)

Descended from a family of lunatics, Baudelaire evidenced his insanity in childhood through his multiple hallucinations and unusual speculations on the horror and ecstasy of life. As he grew older he became more demented, and began acting more impulsively. For example, he loved to throw flower pots from his house at nearby shop windows, and he insisted on changing his residence every month (though perhaps he was forced to). He attempted to strangle his stepfather, lost all his money on a weird trip to India, wore summer clothes in winter—and generally acted as bizarrely as possible. This behavior included his taste in women; he fell madly in love with horrible ugly dwarfs and giantesses. His most common fantasy was that of suspending a woman from the ceiling so that he could kiss and caress her foot.[3]

12 THE BOOK OF LOSERS

9. Guy de Maupassant, French author (1850–1893)

Prone to hallucinations, and depressed about his brother's insanity, Maupassant's mind completely deteriorated near the end of his life. On January 1, 1892, he tried to shoot himself in the head to kill the flies devouring the salt in his brain. Three days later his family had him committed to a Parisian clinic. After spending a year in the asylum, he had turned into an "animal" (according to his doctor). He claimed he was the son of God, became obsessed with piles of eggs, referred to his urine as diamonds, and carried on a continuous dialogue with the devil. He tried to kill fellow inmates with billiard balls, and screamed for hours on end. His misery ended July 6, 1893.[4]

10. Adolf Hitler, German dictator (1889–1945)

Hitler possessed numerous fears, such as fear of dead animals (he became a vegetarian), the moon, and cancer. He was also obsessed with death; when he became Chancellor of Germany he restored beheading by the axe as an official means of execution. A modern-day Caligula, he had filmstrips made of the executions of criminals so he could enjoy watching them die. Of course, Hitler ordered incredible atrocities carried out against all Jews. To cultivate esprit de corps in the SS, he had its members murder Jewish babies in front of their mothers. His gas chambers and crematoria were responsible for the deaths of over 6,000,000 Jews. Moreover, this fascination with blood extended to his personal habits; he enjoyed watching leeches suck out his own blood. His sexual preferences were also quite unusual; he apparently aroused himself with frequent enemas. One of his mistresses reported that he would order her to strip and squat over his head so that she could urinate and defecate on his face.[5]

11. Zelda Fitzgerald, American writer (1901–1948)

Zelda's first signs of mental illness occurred in April 1939, when she had a nervous breakdown—caused by F. Scott's

LOSERS OF BODY FUNCTIONS 13

drinking and carousing with other women. By 1931, her doctors had diagnosed schizophrenia, yet friends felt that her personality had not appreciably changed. Zelda proceeded to be virtually imprisoned in a Swiss sanitarium on her husband's orders; she was unable to write to friends to let them know where she was or to leave as long as her husband paid the bills. In fact, her "mental illness" was based almost entirely on her famous husband's testimony; he claimed she was prone to hysteria and hallucinations. At one point a doctor suggested that F. Scott needed mental treatment more than Zelda, so Scott indignantly had her taken to another doctor, whom he persuaded to commit her again. After a number of years of being carted against her will to asylums, she became genuinely mentally ill and died in a fire in a sanitarium.[6]

SOURCES:
1. *Bible*, 1 Samuel.
2. *Chambers Encyclopaedia*, 1966, vol. 2.
3. Cesare Lombroso, *The Man of Genius*. London: Walter Scott, 1891.
4. Michael Lerner, *Maupassant*. London: George Allen & Unwin Ltd., 1975.
5. Robert Waite, *The Psychopathic God: Adolf Hitler*. New York: Basic Books, 1977.
6. Sara Mayfield, *Exiles from Paradise: Zelda and Scott Fitzgerald*. New York: Delacorte, 1971.

14 THE BOOK OF LOSERS

EXTENDED LOSERS OF CONSCIOUSNESS

Merrily, merrily, merrily, merrily, life is but a dream.
NURSERY JINGLE

No man can lose what he never had.
IZAAK WALTON, *Compleat Angler*

1. Elaine Esposito; Tarpon Springs, Florida

Ms. Esposito was a normal six-year-old child when she entered a Chicago operating room for an appendectomy on August 6, 1941. However, when the operation was over she did not regain consciousness, and lapsed into a coma. She has remained unconscious for thirty-eight years (as of August 1979), and shows no sign of emerging from her sleep. In the meantime, this longest loser of consciousness in history has taken up residence in Florida with her family.[1]

2. Karoline Karlsson; Monsteras, Sweden

Ms. Karlsson's experience began on Christmas Day, 1875, when she was thirteen years old. For reasons that are unclear, she fell unconscious and entered a coma. Her unconsciousness continued for thirty-two years and ninety-nine days, until April 3, 1908. On this date she suddenly awoke. She lived forty-two more years, dying on April 6, 1950, at age eighty-eight.[1]

3. Pyotr Vetrov; Moscow, U.S.S.R.

In December 1942, the twenty-nine-year-old Vetrov was a Red Army truck driver participating in the defense of Moscow. He heard a German shell explode near him—and then nothing.

LOSERS OF BODY FUNCTIONS

Knocked unconscious, he was taken to the Dobrynikha Psychoneurological Clinic, where he entered middle age unconscious. In August 1960, clinicians decided to try a series of electrical shocks to arouse him. After almost eighteen years, Vetrov awoke with the question: "How long have I been asleep?" [2]

4. Robert C. Steger; Louisville, Kentucky

Like most Americans, Steger was engaged in the war effort in February 1943. On the fifth of that month, while at his job at an aeronautical plant near Cincinnati, he was knocked unconscious when a pulley struck him in the head. During the next eight years and eleven months, he reportedly showed no signs of aging, but did gain weight. He died on January 11, 1952, at age sixty-three—never having emerged from his coma. [3]

5. Oscar E. Mills; Gary, Indiana

Mills, an Indiana state patrolman, was in pursuit of a suspect on November 30, 1957. His car apparently went out of control and crashed, leaving Mills unconscious with a skull fracture. The twenty-six-year-old Mills remained in a coma until his death on August 13, 1966. He had been unconscious for eight years and nine months. [4]

6. Beverly Ann Nilsson; New York City

This little girl was critically injured in an automobile accident while on a family outing in Virginia on July 12, 1952. For the next seven and a half years Ms. Nilsson was in a coma. During this period she grew normally, and was exercised in a special box. However, she never responded to any external stimuli except thunder. She died on January 2, 1960. [5]

7. José Rodrigues; New York City

Rodrigues was knocked unconscious on May 15, 1954, in an automobile accident in Philadelphia. He never regained con-

16   *THE BOOK OF LOSERS*

sciousness, dying five years, seven months, and sixteen days later at age forty-five on December 31, 1959.[6]

8. Ralph Abbott; Boston, Massachusetts

In yet another traffic accident, Abbott's car veered off the road near Weston, Massachusetts, plowing into a tree and a stone wall. The impact shattered Abbott's skull and lacerated his brain. Rendered unconscious, he defied the predictions of impending death, and lingered in a coma for five years, seven months, and fourteen days. He died at age thirty-nine, on October 2, 1952.[7]

9. Karen Ann Quinlan; New Jersey

Quinlan's case is interesting not because of the length of her unconsciousness, but because of the legal and moral questions surrounding it. On April 15, 1975, the twenty-one-year-old Ms. Quinlan lapsed into a coma possibly caused by a mixture of Valium and alcohol in her bloodstream. By May 1975, her weight had dropped from 115 to 90 pounds, and doctors felt she was being kept alive by purely artificial means, even though her eyes opened regularly and seemed to move around the room. After a series of trials initiated by her parents' wish to terminate the devices, the U.S. Supreme Court ruled that there would be no criminal liability for doing so. The devices were turned off, but Karen did not die. At present, she has been unconscious for over five years.[8]

10. Carol Rogman; Illinois

In a case similar to Karen Quinlan's, Ms. Rogman survived a terrible automobile accident near her home. However, the crash badly bruised her brain, and doctors gave her a less than 5 percent chance to live. During the period of her coma, she underwent physical changes similar to Quinlan's: her right arm curled over her chest; her legs turned grotesquely under her

LOSERS OF BODY FUNCTIONS 17

body, and her weight dropped from 138 to 65 pounds. Convinced that she had become a vegetable, doctors wanted her removed to a mental hospital, but her mother refused. After four months in a deep coma, she began to emerge in January 1967. She later returned to normal, married, and had children.[9]

SOURCES:
1. Norris McWhirter, ed., 1978 edition: *Guinness Book of World Records*. New York: Bantam, 1977.
2. *Newsweek*, Aug. 15, 1960.
3. *New York Times*, January 12, 1952.
4. *New York Times*, April 14, 1966.
5. *New York Times*, January 3, 1960.
6. *New York Times*, January 1, 1960.
7. *New York Times*, October 3, 1952.
8. *Reader's Digest*, May, 1978.
9. *Good Housekeeping*, June, 1976.

NOTABLE LOSERS OF WEIGHT

There are occasions when it is undoubtedly better to incur loss than to make gain.

PLAUTUS, *Captivi*

1. Jon Brower Minnoch

When firemen answered a call in March 1978, they discovered the corpulent six-foot-one Minnoch in his second-story apartment. Unable to move or speak, Minnoch was too large to be carried out his door and had to be lowered to the ground through a second-story window. At the hospital, doctors did not have scales that could give his precise weight; however, they determined that he weighed in excess of 1,400 pounds—over 300

18   THE BOOK OF LOSERS

pounds heavier than the heaviest recorded man. Placed on a diet, Minnoch had succeeded in losing over 900 pounds (he weighed 475) as of July 1979.[1]

2. William J. Cobb

Cobb, a professional wrestler from Macon, Georgia, known as "Happy Humphrey," overwhelmed his opponents with his 802-pound bulk and 101-inch waist. Perhaps unhappy with his appearance in wrestling trunks, Cobb began a diet that resulted in his losing 570 pounds—down to 232 by July 1965. For whatever reason, Cobb's new 44-inch waist must not have been satisfying because at last report he had regained over 400 pounds.[1]

3. Wanda Bork

Mrs. Bork realized that something had to be done when she could only draw two inches of water for her bath, and her stomach touched the floor when she sat. She proceeded to join Weight Watchers and went to work on her 541 pounds. Three years later, on February 20, 1978, the Sanger, California, housewife had lost 402 pounds—reaching her goal of 139 pounds. So inspired was her family that her daughter lost 65 pounds and her husband lost 90 pounds.[2]

4. Mrs. Celesta Geyer

Forced by a heart attack at age forty-nine to embark on a reducing program, Cincinnati circus fat lady Mrs. Geyer, known as "Dolly Dimples," began an 800-calorie-a-day diet. By July 18, 1951, Mrs. Geyer had reduced from 553 pounds to 152 pounds—a loss of 401 pounds. Simultaneously, her measurements were transformed from 79–84–84 to 34–28–36.[3]

LOSERS OF BODY FUNCTIONS   19

5. Paul M. Kimelman
Mr. Kimelman strictly limited his caloric intake to a maximum of 600 calories a day to reduce his weight by a remarkable 357 pounds in eight months. During this period between January and August 1967, the Pittsburg native slimmed from 487 to 130 pounds.[1]

6. Mrs. Gertrude Levandowski
Mrs. Levandowski undertook a more radical form of weight loss—a series of operations designed to shorten her digestive tract. These operations were spectacularly successful for the 616-pound Burnips, Michigan, resident. She cut her weight in half by losing 308 pounds.[1]

7. Craig Hiller
Taking yet another form of weight reduction, Mr. Hiller, a Cleveland interior decorator, gained fame by fasting away his pounds. In five months he lost 141 pounds on a diet of alanine (amino acid), glucose, and water or diet drinks. During this period his weight dropped from 341 to 200 pounds.[4]

8. Mrs. Helen Federowicz
In a rather bizarre chapter in the history of weight reducing, Mrs. Federowicz was forced to march her pounds away. Unhappy with his plump wife, John Federowicz decided to take Helen on a short trek. Four months and 2,000 miles later, Mrs. Federowicz's diet was immensely successful, as she trimmed from 265 to 155 pounds: a loss of 110 pounds. For those interested in following the Federowiczes' diet, they walked from Fresno, California, over the mountains and deserts to the Mexican border.[5]

9. Mrs. Jean Nidetch

Perhaps the most famous weight loser is Mrs. Nidetch, who became so involved with losing weight that she began holding meetings with neighbors while she was reducing. After her own successful reduction, from 214 pounds to 142, Mrs. Nidetch founded Weight Watchers, which has given hope to weight losers everywhere.[6]

SOURCES:

1. Norris McWhirter, ed., 1978 edition: *Guinness Book of World Records.* New York: Bantam, 1977.
2. *Good Housekeeping,* August, 1978.
3. *New York Times,* July 19, 1951.
4. *Time,* Nov. 22, 1976.
5. *New York Times,* Aug. 10, 1953.
6. *McCall's,* May, 1970.

PEOPLE WHO LOST THEIR SIGHT

O loss of sight, of thee I most complain!
Blind among enemies, O worse than chains,
Dungeon, or beggary, or decrepit age!
JOHN MILTON: *Samson Agonistes*

1. Samson, Israelite hero (c. 1100 B.C.)

After being seduced and shaved by Delilah, Samson fell prey to the Philistines, who plucked out his eyes. They then took him to Gaza, where they made sacrifices to their god Dagon for delivering them from such an enemy. They became complacent

LOSERS OF BODY FUNCTIONS 21

in their rejoicing, however, and ordered that Samson be brought to the temple for sport. Sensing a chance to redeem himself, Samson asked his guide to direct him to the main pillars of the building. He then prayed that he might be avenged of his blindness. God answered his prayers, and Samson pulled down the building—killing himself and 3,000 Philistines (Judges 16:21–30).

2. Homer, Greek poet (c. 850 B.C.)

Nothing is known concerning the origins of Homer's blindness. Presumably he was completely sightless when he dictated the *Iliad* and the *Odyssey* to a scribe.

3. Ossian, Caledonian bard (3rd century B.C.)

The son of King Fingal lost his sight in battle, and spent the remainder of his life wandering about the countryside singing songs of battle and of man's freedom.

4. Didymus, Eastern church theologian (c. 313–398)

After having lost his sight at four or five years of age, Didymus carved his own alphabet of letters out of a piece of wood. He soon learned how to form words and make sentences. Didymus continued to teach himself, and became one of the greatest intellects of the ancient world; he followed Origen as head of the renowned Catechetical School of Alexandria.

5. Abdu'l Ala al Ma'arri, Arab religious skeptic and poet (973–?)

At the age of four, Abdu'l lost his sight as the result of a horrible case of smallpox. Undaunted and determined to become a scholar, he proceeded to memorize the contents of the three great libraries of Haleb, Antioch, and Tripoli. He went on to

22   THE BOOK OF LOSERS

become a leading religious skeptic and poet. It has been said that he marked the zenith of Arab poetry of the time.

6. Prospero Fagnani, Italian canonist and theologian (1588–1678)

Prospero attained the degree of doctor of civil and canon law when he was only twenty-one. At the age of forty-four blindness struck, but he continued his intense canonical studies. Finally in 1661 he was ready to write his masterpiece, *Commentary on the Decretals of Gregory IX*. This book was recognized by scholars everywhere as the clearest interpretation of, and final authority on, the most complex and disputed questions of canon law.

7. John Milton, English scholar and poet (1608–1674)

Like Fagnani, Milton achieved distinction before he lost his sight. In fact, it was his seven years in residence at Cambridge that is considered the cause of his blindness (he habitually studied in poor light). Of course, after he became blind, he wrote his greatest poetry, *Paradise Lost*.

8. Nicholas Saunderson, English mathematician (1682–1739)

Saunderson had the misfortune to lose his sight because of smallpox when he was four years old. However, his father sent him to an academy for non-handicapped students, where he quickly displayed an incredible aptitude in mathematics. While there, Saunderson developed a ciphering board (still used today) on which he could solve problems with lightning speed. Denied permission to enter Cambridge because of his blindness, he was nonetheless allowed to conduct a class on the principles of Sir Isaac Newton—since he was one of the few men who could understand him. At Newton's insistence, Queen Anne bestowed a degree on Saunderson which allowed him to become the Lucasian Professor of Mathematics at Cambridge.

LOSERS OF BODY FUNCTIONS   23

9. François Huber, Swiss apiarist (1750–1831)

Cataracts took Huber's sight before he was sixteen; yet he continued to attend lectures at the University of Geneva. However, he soon had to retire to the countryside because of poor health. At this point he began to study bees. Through listening to the bees' humming, he discovered the nuptial flight, the bees' use of antennae, the genesis of swarms, and the meaning of periodic bee migrations. At the time of his death, Huber was the foremost apiarist in the world.

10. Louis Braille, French educator (1809–1852)

At the age of three, Braille was playing in his father's leather shop when his knife slipped and plunged into his eye. He was immediately blinded in that eye and soon lost sight in his other eye due to sympathetic ophthalmia. Twelve years later, he adapted a system of reading by raised dots for use by the blind, and later adapted it to musical notation. In 1826, he became a professor at the French National Institute for Blind Youth, a post he kept until his death.

11. Jorge Luis Borges, Argentinian writer (1899–)

This poet and novelist became completely blind after he had achieved a measure of fame at the age of fifty-six. Nonetheless, his most acclaimed works have come after his blindness, including *The Book of Imaginary Beings*, in which Borges breaks down the barriers between prose and poetry.

Primary source: Gabriel Farrell, *The Story of Blindness*. Harvard: Harvard Univ. Cambridge, Mass. Press, 1956.

24   THE BOOK OF LOSERS

People Who Totally Lost Their Hearing

None is so deaf as who will not hear.
Thomas Ingeland, *Disobedient Child*

1. Lord Chesterfield, Philip Dormer Stanhope, English statesman (1694–1773)

Stanhope's deafness struck suddenly during the early months of 1752. All remedies having failed, he retired to his estate, where he remained until his death, still the center of a great cultural environment.[1]

2. Francisco Goya, Spanish artist (1746–1828)

In 1793 an attack of paralysis left Goya completely deaf at the age of forty-seven. The loss seemed to make his powers of observation even more acute; he wrote that it was like seeing the world for the first time. In the remaining thirty-five years of his life he created some of his most important works, including his famous "Family of Charles IV," and his etching, "The Disasters of War."[2]

3. Ludwig van Beethoven, German composer (1770–1827)

Beethoven became totally deaf in 1817; numerous biographers have postulated the probable causes. Beethoven himself told a friend that he was writing an opera when he was disturbed by a tenor. He flew into a rage, and "I threw myself on the floor as actors do, and when I arose I found myself deaf." Whatever the cause, Beethoven's deafness did not stop him from composing three piano sonatas, the "Diabelli" Variations, and the triumphant Ninth Symphony.[3]

LOSERS OF BODY FUNCTIONS

4. Bedřich Smetana, Czechoslovakian composer (1824–1884)

Smetana became totally deaf in 1874; however, he continued to compose until his death. Many of his most famous compositions were written after he became deaf, including his intensely nationalistic symphonic poems, *My Country*, and a string quartet, *From My Life*.[4]

SOURCES:
1. W.H. Craig, *Life of Lord Chesterfield*. London: John Lane, 1907.
2. Arnold Vallentin, *This I Saw: The Life and Times of Goya*. New York: Random House, 1949.
3. Primary Source: Emil Ludwig, *Beethoven: Life of a Conqueror*. New York: G.P. Putnam's Sons, 1943.
4. Brian Large, *Smetana*. New York: Praeger, 1970.

LOSERS OF NOSES

'Tis said that people ought to guard their noses
Who thrust them into matters none of theirs.
THOMAS HOOD, *Ode to Roe Wilson*

To cut off one's nose to spite one's face.
PUBLILIUS SYRUS, *Sententiae*

1. Tycho Brahe, Danish astronomer (1546–1601)

The noted Brahe lost a portion of his nose in a sword fight to resolve a mathematical dispute; he had it replaced with a gold and silver one.

26 THE BOOK OF LOSERS

2. Josef Myslivecek, Czechoslovakian composer (1737–1781)
Afflicted with a severe case of venereal disease in 1787, Myslivecek visited a quack physician who suggested that he could be cured by a simple nose amputation. Desperate for relief, the composer agreed to the operation.

Source: David Wallechinsky and Irving Wallace, *The People's Almanac #2*. New York: Bantam, 1978.

LOSERS OF ARMS OR HANDS

Let him value his hands and feet, he has but one pair.
EMERSON, *Conduct of Life, Fate*

1. Miguel de Cervantes, Spanish author of *Don Quixote* (1547–1616)
A professional soldier before becoming a writer, Cervantes had his left hand blown off fighting against the Turks at the Battle of Lepanto on October 7, 1571. He later remarked that his left hand was destroyed "to the greater glory of the right."[1]

2. Horatio Nelson, English naval officer (1785–1805)
Nelson's ship, the *Theseus*, was badly beaten on July 24, 1797, while attacking several Spanish treasure ships. During the battle, grapeshot shattered Nelson's right elbow; his arm had to be amputated. When he was asked if he wanted the arm preserved, he said, "Throw it into the hammock with the brave fellow that was killed beside me."[2]

LOSERS OF BODY FUNCTIONS 27

3. Thomas Jonathan (Stonewall) Jackson, Confederate general (1824–1863)

While reconnoitering the enemy, Jackson was accidentally shot by his own troops on May 2, 1863. His left arm was amputated immediately; he died eight days later of pneumonia.[3]

4. Hugh "One Arm" Daly, major-league pitcher for seven teams (1857– ?)

Daly appeared in 164 games during the years 1882 through 1887, despite having only one arm. In this period his best year was 1883, when he had a 24–18 record for Cleveland. He posted a lifetime 74–88 record, including a no-hitter and a game in which he struck out nineteen batters, a major-league record.[4]

5. James Stacy, actor

The 1978 Academy Award nominee lost his left arm and leg when his motorcycle was hit by a drunken driver September 27, 1973. In 1976 he won a $1.9 million suit against the tavern that served the driver the drinks.[5]

SOURCES:
1. *Encyclopaedia Britannica*, 1974, vol. 3.
2. Ernie Bradford, *Nelson: The Essential Hero*. New York: Harcourt, Brace, Jovanovich, 1977.
3. *Encyclopaedia Britannica*, 1974, vol. 10.
4. Hy Turkin, S.C. Thompson, and Pete Palmer, *The Official Encyclopedia of Baseball (9th ed.)*. Garden City, N.Y.: Dolphin, 1977.
5. *Los Angeles Times*, May 5, 1976.

LOSERS OF LEGS

Uxbridge: "By God, sir, I've lost my leg!"
Wellington: "By God, sir, so you have!"
(reported exchange at Waterloo, on the
occasion of the Earl of Uxbridge having a
French cannonball blow off his leg while
he was talking to Wellington)

1. Peter Stuyvesant, Dutch soldier and official (1610–1672)

While participating in a 1644 campaign against the Portuguese in the West Indies, Stuyvesant was severely wounded in his right leg. It was amputated and replaced with a silver-ornamented wooden one. [1]

2. Antonio Lopez de Santa Anna, Mexican general (1795–1876)

The Mexican general lost his leg in an 1838 battle in Veracruz against French warships. To celebrate his birthday in 1842, Santa Anna had the leg dug up from its resting place at Manga de Clavo and carried in a grand procession to the capital, where it was enshrined in an urn at the cemetery of Santa Paula. [2]

3. Sarah Bernhardt, French actress (1844–1923)

In 1886 on a voyage from South America to the United States, Bernhardt had a bad fall and severely injured her right knee. In 1891 she suffered another disastrous injury to the knee when she missed the mattress after leaping to the stage in the final act of *Tosca*. By 1915 her knee had grown so bad that she always wore a cast; in February, gangrene was dicovered. On February 22,

LOSERS OF BODY FUNCTIONS 29

1915, the Divine Sarah's right leg was amputated in a hospital near Bordeaux. P. T. Barnum offered her $10,000 to let him display the severed leg in a freak show; she graciously refused.[3]

4. Cole Porter, American songwriter (1892–1964)

For over twenty years, Porter suffered the painful effects of a horse-riding accident which occurred in 1937 (at the time, doctors wanted to amputate both legs). On April 3, 1958, doctors decided to amputate his right leg to the hip because it was badly ulcerated and the smell of rotting flesh indicated a threat to his life.[4]

5. Al Capp, cartoonist, creator of Li'l Abner (1909–1979)

At the age of twelve, Capp was severely injured in a New Haven, Connecticut, street car accident. As a result, doctors were forced to amputate his right leg.[5]

6. Totie Fields, American comedienne (1931–1978)

On April 22, 1976, the performer's left leg was amputated because of severe phlebitis.[6]

7. Max Cleland, director of Veterans Administration

On April 8, 1968, at Khe Sanh, South Vietnam, a Viet Cong hand grenade blew off both of Cleland's legs and his right arm.[7]

8. Edward Kennedy, Jr. (1962–)

The son of the Massachusetts senator had his right leg amputated in November 1973, after it was discovered he had bone cancer.[8]

9. Josip Broz Tito, Yugoslavian president (1893–1980)

The eighty-seven-year-old Tito entered Ljubljana Medical Clinic on January 3, 1980. Because doctors were unable to

30 *THE BOOK OF LOSERS*

bypass a blood clot in his left leg, it was amputated two weeks later.[9]

SOURCES:
1. *Encyclopedia Americana*, 1976, vol. 25.
2. Oakah Jones, *Santa Anna*. New York: Twayne Publishers, 1968.
3. Cornelia Skinner, *Madame Sarah*. Boston: Houghton Mifflin, 1967.
4. Richard Hulder, *The Cole Porter Story*. New York: World Pub. Co., 1965.
5. *Current Biography, 1947*. New York: H.W. Wilson, 1948.
6. *San Francisco Chronicle*, April 23, 1976.
7. Primary Source: *Rolling Stone*, February 9, 1978.
8. *Los Angeles Times*, November 18, 1973.
9. *Time*, February 4, 1980.

PEOPLE WHO LOST THE USE OF A LIMB OR LIMBS

We must have you find your legs.
SHAKESPEARE, II *Henry* VI

1. Peter the Gouty, Florentine leader (1416–1469)

Son of the great Cosimo de Medici, Peter ascended to the leadership of Florence upon Cosimo's death in 1464. He gained his appelation "the Gouty" when he became so crippled by gout that during his last years he could move only his tongue.[1]

2. Mary, Queen of Scots (1542–1587)

Rheumatoid arthritis slowly devastated the queen's body, first attacking her neck, then moving to her hands and elbows. For several years she was a complete cripple, unable to even turn in

LOSERS OF BODY FUNCTIONS 31

her bed. Mysteriously, the disease went into remission shortly before her death.[1]

3. James Madison, 4th U.S. President (1751–1836)
By 1832 Madison's shoulders, wrists, fingers, and feet were so crippled by arthritis that he had to be laid on a couch to conduct business interviews.[1]

4. Sir Walter Scott, English author (1771–1832)
An at early age, the novelist lost the use of his right leg because of polio.[2]

5. Pierre Auguste Renoir, French Impressionist artist (1841–1919)
Suffering from severe rheumatoid arthritis from 1897 to his death in 1919, Renoir continued painting despite the virtual loss of his hands and wrists to the disease.[1]

6. Franklin Roosevelt, 32nd U.S. President (1884–1945)
Infantile paralysis struck Roosevelt on the morning of August 11, 1921. Five months later, he was forced to wear braces, and he was never able to walk unsupported again.[3]

7. George C. Wallace, Alabama governor (1919–)
The presidential candidate was paralyzed from the waist down by a bullet from Arthur Bremer's gun while campaigning in Laurel, Maryland, on Mary 15, 1972.[4]

8. Roy Campanella, Dodgers baseball player (1921–)
On January 28, 1958, Campanella's car skidded out of control on an icy New York road, and into a telephone pole. The crash fractured and dislocated Campanella's vertebrae and broke his neck, permanently paralyzing him from the chest down.[5]

32 THE BOOK OF LOSERS

9. Maurice Stokes, Cincinnati Royals basketball player (1934–)

The six-foot-seven Stokes collapsed on the Royals' team airplane on March 15, 1958—apparently of a brain infection. He remained in a coma for days; when he regained consciousness, he was permanently paralyzed.[6]

10. Stephen Hawking, Cambridge research physicist (1942–)

Hawking, who is the foremost black-hole theorist, has been described as an intellectual equal to Einstein. As of 1978, he was unable to even raise his head without great difficulty and was completely confined to a wheelchair—a victim of amyotrophic lateral sclerosis.[7]

SOURCES:
1. W.S.C. Copeman, *A Short History of the Gout and the Rheumatic Diseases*. Berkeley: Univ. of California Press, 1964.
2. J.F. Nisbet, *The Insanity of Genius*. London: Grant Richards, 1900.
3. Kenneth S. Davis, *FDR: The Beckoning of Destiny*. New York: G.P. Putnam's Sons, 1971.
4. *Washington Post*, May 16, 1972.
5. Primary Source: *New York Times*, January 29, 1958.
6. *Saturday Evening Post*, March 14, 1959.
7. *Time*, September 4, 1978.

LOSERS OF BODY FUNCTIONS

MEN WHO LOST THEIR PENISES

He that is wounded in the stones, or hath his privy member cut off, shall not enter into the congregation of the Lord.

DEUTERONOMY 23:1

1. Combabus, servant to Assyrian Queen Stratonice-Semiramis (2000 B.C.)

Upon being ordered by the king to accompany Stratonice to Hierapolis, Combabus suspected that the jealous king would soon become suspicious. To dispel future worries, Combabus secretly cut off his penis and placed it in a sealed vessel which he gave to the king. Three years later the king proved jealous as ever and ordered Combabus executed on the grounds of suspected intimacy with Stratonice. However, Combabus proceeded to produce the vessel and save his life.

2. Kang Ping, Chinese general under Ming Emperor Young Lo (c. 1410)

This patron saint of eunuchs was ordered by the emperor to take charge of the castle while he was away. Kang Ping had possibly heard of Combabus, for he too excised his penis and placed it in the hollow of the emperor's saddle—and so saved his life when he was later accused of adulterous relations with the empress. Young Lo was so impressed with Kang Ping's deed that he made him chief eunuch, and deified Kang when he died.

3. Pannovius, Greek eunuch tradesman (490 B.C.)

Pannovius made his drachma by selling young boys he had castrated to the Persians. However, one of his victims, Hermontinus the Pedasian, eventually rose to power in the court of

34   THE BOOK OF LOSERS

Xerxes. He subsequently participated in Xerxes's campaign against Greece, during which he trapped Pannovius's four sons on the isle of Chios and castrated them. To add insult to injury, he then forced the sons to emasculate their father Pannovius.

4. 43,430 anonymous Libyans, Philistines, and Khwarazmians

(1) 1300 B.C.: After successfully stopping an invasion by Libyans, Egyptian King Meneptah had the penises of 13,230 Libyan soldiers removed, including those of six Libyan generals. (2) 1000 B.C.: To impress his future father-in-law, David presented Saul (first king of Israel) with 200 Philistine penises. (3) Noting the elasticity and durability of the skin of the scrotum, Sultan Key Coubad I ordered the penises and scrotums of 30,000 enemy Khwarazmians removed and sewn together to produce tents for his army. The process took five days.

5. Sporus, Roman eunuch (c. A.D. 50)

Possessed of beautiful face and body, this castrated courtesan had the dubious fortune of infatuating Nero. In fact, Nero was so infatuated that he staged an elaborate wedding with himself as the groom and Sporus as the bride. To the horror of more refined sensibilities, Nero constantly strolled the Via Flaminia with his lover, caressing him at every opportunity.

6. Peter Abelard, Abbot of St. Gildas-de-Rhuys (1079–1142)

Angered because Abelard had seduced and impregnated his niece Heloise, Fulbert and his kinsmen schemed for revenge against the abbot. One night when Abelard was asleep they bribed his servant, burst in upon him, and cut off his penis; according to Abelard, "they deprived me of that part of my body with which I had committed the deeds of which they complained."

LOSERS OF BODY FUNCTIONS 35

7. Roger de Mortimer, French courtier (?–1330)

Mortimer and Isabel of France became engaged in a searing love affair; to facilitate their meetings they planned and carried out the murder of Isabel's husband, Edward II, in 1326. For several years they lived in bliss at Castle Rising near Lynn, France, until the new king, Edward III, asserted his independence in 1330. Isabel was forced into a nunnery; Mortimer was castrated, and later executed.

8. William Parry, attorney; Thomas Babington, courtier; Ruy Lopez, physician

During the period between 1585 and 1595, these three men were all convicted of conspiring against Queen Elizabeth I. The sentence of the court read that the prisoners were to have their "privy parts cut off," then they were to be disemboweled and their entrails burned before their eyes (which they all survived); finally, they were to be killed—by quartering. In all three instances, the sentences were executed to the letter of the law.

9. Girolamo Rossini, Italian singer (c. 1600)

Rossini was the first castrato to sing in the papal choir. After being castrated, Rossini's voice was so tender and could achieve such high notes that other members of the choir forced him to resign. He then became a Franciscan friar, but Pope Clement VIII so loved his voice that he ordered Rossini back. So began the tradition of obtaining castrated males for the papal choir; the practice continued until an 1851 papal bull abolished the castration of singers. Nonetheless, such singers remained in the choir until as late as 1922.

10. George Jorgensen, American photographer (1926–)

On September 24, 1951, George Jorgensen underwent the first of three operations to make him the first transsexual in history.

THE BOOK OF LOSERS

On November 22, 1952, Danish doctors performed a penectomy, and George Jorgensen became Christine Jorgensen, nightclub entertainer.

11. Richard Raskind, U.S. tennis player (1935–)

In August 1975, Raskind, a successful ophthalmologist, amateur tennis player, husband, and father, had his penis surgically removed and became Renee Richards. Shortly thereafter she aroused a storm of controversy by playing on the women's tennis tour.

Primary source: Peter Tompkins, *The Eunuch and the Virgin*. New York: Bramhall House, 1962.

–II–
Losers of Life

I'm not afraid to die. I just don't want to be there when it happens.

WOODY ALLEN

TEN JOBS IN WHICH YOU ARE MOST LIKELY TO ACCIDENTALLY LOSE YOUR LIFE

	Deaths Over the National Average per 1,000 per year
Astronaut	30 (est.)
Driver of Gold Cup hydroplane	25 (est.)
Driver of Indianapolis race car	25 (est.)
Driver in Grand Prix auto race	25 (est.)
Aerial performer (without net)	8 (est.)
Professional prizefighter	8 (est.)
Lumberman or woodchopper in the Pacific area	6.18
Professional diver (helmet or skin)	4 (est.)
Electrical power line constructor, tower erector, or lineman	3.44
Steeplejacks	2.78

Source: *1967 Occupational Study.* Chicago: Society of Actuaries.

TEN STATES IN WHICH YOU ARE MOST LIKELY TO LOSE YOUR LIFE ACCIDENTALLY (1970)

State	Rate per 100,000
Alaska	117.2
Wyoming	100.2
New Mexico	89.1
Idaho	82.9
Mississippi	81.6
Montana	81.1
Arizona	75.9
Alabama	74.8
Nevada	74.7
Georgia	73.7

Source: Statistical Bureau of the Metropolitan Life Insurance Company.

ELEVEN COUNTRIES WHOSE INHABITANTS ARE MOST LIKELY TO LOSE THEIR LIVES BY ACCIDENTAL CAUSES (PER 100,000 POPULATION)

South Africa (Blacks)	88.0
France	74.8
South Africa (Whites)	70.9
Réunion	70.4

LOSERS OF LIFE

Austria	69.8
Portugal	63.0
Luxembourg	62.6
Guadaloupe	61.7
Belgium	60.1
Hungary	58.8
Canada	57.6

Note: South Africa reports black and white population statistics separately.
Source: United Nations Demographic Yearbook, 1977.

TEN STATES IN WHICH YOU ARE MOST LIKELY TO LOSE YOUR LIFE IN A CAR (1977)

State	*Rate per 100,000,000 vehicle miles*
New Mexico	5.9
Wyoming	5.4
Nevada	5.1
Arizona	5.1
Montana	5.0
Idaho	5.0
Louisiana	4.5
Mississippi	4.3
West Virginia	4.3
South Carolina	4.1

Source: National Safety Council.

SIXTEEN COUNTRIES IN WHICH YOU ARE MOST LIKELY TO LOSE YOUR LIFE IN A CAR (1975)

Country	Rate per 100,000 registered motor vehicles
Poland	164
Greece	160
Hungary	134
Czechoslovakia	117
Austria	104
Ireland	97
Spain	83
West Germany	71
Belgium	68
Finland	66
France	61
Denmark	53
Italy	50
Switzerland	46
Norway	44
East Germany	44

Source: National Highway Traffic Safety Administration.

TEN FAMOUS PEOPLE WHO LOST THEIR LIVES IN AUTOMOBILE ACCIDENTS

Here lies G. Whilkin's friends, all five,
He took them along when he learned to drive.

LEONARD ROBBINS, *Epitaphs for the Space Age*

1. Isadora Duncan, American dancer (1878–1927)

Isadora decided to take a trial ride down the French coast near Nice in a small Bugatti sports car that she wanted to buy (she also had a romantic interest in its driver, Benoit Falchetto). As she was about to step into the front seat, she turned to her friends and cried: "Adieu, mes amis, je vais a la gloire!" ("Good-bye, my friends, I'm off to glory!") Before Falchetto started the car, she was seen to throw over her left shoulder the long-fringed end of a red silk shawl which was wrapped twice around her neck. Falchetto then pushed the accelerator quickly, and the car thrust forward with the shawl trailing alongside. Almost as quickly, Falchetto stopped the car, presumably to allow Isadora to pick up the shawl. However, in the space of seconds, the end of the shawl had been wound twice around the wheel, crushing Isadora's larynx, breaking her neck, and causing her carotid artery to burst—instantly killing her.[1]

2. Pierre Michelin, French industrialist

Michelin died instantly from injuries received in the early morning crash of his special Citroën automobile near Montargis, France, on December 30, 1937. The exact cause of the crash

42　　*THE BOOK OF LOSERS*

was never determined, but police had reason to believe that it resulted from a defective mechanism in the car he was driving. As well as being a high official in the Michelin Tire Company, he was also the managing director of the Citroën Automobile Company.[2]

3. General George S. Patton, Jr., American general (1885–1945)

Patton was going out for his weekly Sunday morning pheasant shoot, in his seven-seater 1938 Cadillac '75 Special Limousine, on his final day before returning to the United States. He was sitting in the right rear seat beside his hunting dog and General Gay. As the car neared Mannheim at a speed of about 30 mph, an Army GMC truck pulled out of a side road, and squarely hit the right side of the car bed, throwing Patton forward. The lowered glass partition took all the skin from his forehead, partially scalped him, and completely separated his spinal column. Yet the sixty-year-old general never even lost consciousness, and according to his driver he began to "swear a little." Paralyzed from his neck down, the general was taken to a nearby hospital, where he steadily recovered, gradually regaining the use of various parts of his body. Around the 18th of December, he received the devastating news that he would never be able to ride his horse again, and on the 20th he suffered an embolism of the lung. Several times on the 21st he told his nurse he was going to die, and at 5:55 P.M. he did.[3]

4. Margaret Mitchell, American author of *Gone With the Wind* (1900–1949)

Mitchell and her husband John were back in Atlanta after a New York vacation, and were on their way to see a movie. At 8:20 P.M. they parked their car on Peachtree Street, and began to cross. As they reached halfway, a car suddenly careened around a

LOSERS OF LIFE 43

blind curve up the street. Margaret drew back as the driver jammed on his brakes; however, the car skidded into her and knocked her down near the curb she had just left. Despite terrible head injuries, she survived in a coma for five days. Mitchell died on August 16, 1949, never having regained consciousness.[4]

5. James Dean, American actor (1931–1955)
Around 5:30 P.M. on September 30, 1955, Dean was traveling at about 85 mph west on California 466 out of Bakersfield in his silver Porsche Spyder. A Ford sedan going in the opposite direction on 466 began to turn left, crossing into Dean's path. Dean did not even have time to brake the car and they crashed, leaving the Porsche looking like "a crumpled pack of cigarettes." Dean, trapped in the front seat behind the wheel, was virtually decapitated; his head was left hanging over the driver's door. He died instantly of a broken neck.[5]

6. Jackson Pollock, American artist (1912–1956)
After a day of drinking beer, Pollock was speeding north toward his home at East Hampton, Long Island, at approximately 10:15 P.M. on August 11, 1956. He lost control of his convertible on a sharp curve a short distance from his house. The car plunged off the road, crashed into an embankment, then plowed through 175 feet of underbrush before smashing into a group of white oak trees. The final impact caused the car to turn end over end and land upside down. Pollock was thrown clear of the car, but he was killed instantly when his head hit a tree. Cause of death: compound skull fracture, brain and lung laceration, shock.[6]

7. Aly Khan (1911–1960)
The son and heir to the incredible Aga Khan was driving his custom Lancia down Parisian side streets near the Seine on May

44 THE BOOK OF LOSERS

12, 1960. As he approached a slow-moving Renault from behind, he decided to accelerate past the car on the left. His Lancia had just pulled alongside the Renault when a yellow Simca Aronde suddenly appeared in the same lane ahead. Each person in the resulting collision survived, with the exception of Khan, who died instantly.[6]

8. Albert Camus, French writer (1913–1960)

Camus was traveling back to Paris from the south of France in his Facel-Vega on January 5, 1960. Nearing the little country town of Petit-Villeblevin, his car, which was traveling at a high speed, skidded off the road and hit a tree. Camus died instantly.[8]

9. Jayne Mansfield, American actress (1932–1967)

On the night of June 30, 1967, Mansfield left a Biloxi, Mississippi, nightclub to make a two-hour trip to New Orleans for a television appearance. On the outskirts of New Orleans, city crews were spraying mosquito insecticide into the mist; this caused a large trailer truck to slow down because of poor visibility. Traveling in the same direction as the truck on U.S. 90, Mansfield's car rounded a curve at high speed and smashed into the rear end of it. The force of the crash sheared back the top of the car and decapitated Miss Mansfield, who was in the front right seat.[9]

10. Mary Jo Kopechne, Kennedy political worker (1941–1969)

The facts in this case are shrouded in mystery. At some point on the night of July 18, 1969, Ms. Kopechne died in a car driven by Senator Edward Kennedy. The 1967 Oldsmobile he was driving plunged thirty-six feet through the air off a small bridge on Chappaquiddick Island, Massachusetts, and landed upside down in eight feet of water. The cause of death (drowning or asphyxiation) was never firmly established. After rigor mortis had set in, Ms. Kopechne was found holding onto the front edge of

LOSERS OF LIFE

the back seat with her head thrust to the ceiling in an apparent attempt to get air. According to the coroner, she was wearing a white long-sleeved blouse, dark slacks, a blue brassiere, but no panties.[10]

SOURCES:
1. Allan R. Macdougall, *Isadora: A Revolutionary in Art and Love*. New York: Thomas Nelson & Sons, 1960.
2. *New York Times*, December 31, 1937.
3. Martin Blumenson, *The Patton Papers*. Boston: Houghton Mifflin, 1974.
4. Finis Farr, *Margaret Mitchell of Atlanta*. New York: William Morrow, 1965.
5. David Dalton, *James Dean: The Mutant King*. San Francisco: Simon & Schuster, 1974.
6. Bernard Friedman, *Jackson Pollock: Energy Made Visible*. New York: McGraw Hill, 1972.
7. *New York Times*, May 13, 1960.
8. *New York Times*, January 5, 1960.
9. *New York Times*, June 30, 1967.
10. Robert Sherrill, *The Last Kennedy*. New York: The Dial Press, 1976.

ELEVEN GREATEST LOSSES OF LIFE DUE TO AIRPLANE CRASHES

Lives Lost	*Date/Location/Circumstances*
582	March 27, 1977; Tenerife, Canary Islands: a KLM 747, which had been forced to the airport because of a guerrilla attack elsewhere, collided on takeoff with a Pan American 747 going across the runway.
346	March 3, 1974; Paris, France: The rear cargo door of a Turkish DC-10 burst open shortly after takeoff, causing a loss of control; the plane crashed into a forest north of Paris.
272	May 25, 1979; Chicago, Illinois: After losing an engine shortly after takeoff, an American Airlines

THE BOOK OF LOSERS

	DC-10 crashed. Three more persons died on the ground in this worst ever U.S. crash.
213	January 1, 1978; Bombay, India: An Air India 747 exploded and crashed.
191	December 4, 1974; Maskelia, Sri Lanka: With visibility limited by heavy rains, a Dutch DC-8 carrying Indonesian Moslems on a pilgrimage to Mecca crashed in the mountains near the town.
188	August 3, 1975; Agadir, Morocco: Ten minutes before the chartered plane's scheduled landing with a group of vacationing Moroccans, the Boeing 707 crashed in heavy fog in the Atlas Mountains.
183	November 25, 1978; Colombo, Sri Lanka: A charter Icelandic DC-8 went down in a thunderstorm.
176	October 13, 1972; Moscow, U.S.S.R.: For unknown reasons, the Soviet Ilyushin jet (Aeroflot) circled the field of Sheremetyevo Airport three times before suddenly slamming into the ground near a small village nearby.
176	January 22, 1973; Kano, Nigeria: Attempting to land on a fog-enveloped runway, the Jordanian Airlines Boeing 707 (returning from Mecca with Moslem pilgrims) missed the runway by forty feet, ran into a ditch, and exploded.
176	September 10, 1976; Zagreb, Yugoslavia: Due to poor directions from air traffic controllers, there was a midair collision between a British Trident and a Yugoslavian DC-9.
173	August 17, 1979; Ukraine, U.S.S.R.: Little is known of this crash. According to official reports, two Soviet Aeroflot jet liners collided in midair.

Primary source: James Cornell, *The Great International Disaster Book*. New York: Charles Scribner's Sons, 1976.

FAMOUS PEOPLE WHO LOST THEIR LIVES IN AIRPLANE CRASHES

Americans have an abiding belief in their ability to control reality by purely material means. Hence . . . airline insurance replaces the fear of death with the comforting prospect of cash.

CECIL BEATON

1. Roald Amundsen, Norwegian explorer (1872–1928)
Details are sketchy, but Amundsen's partner in a previous polar adventure, the Italian Umberto Nobile, had crashed his dirigible near Spitzbergen, Norway. Amundsen took off to rescue him, but his plane went down over rough Arctic seas on June 18, 1928. No trace of him or his plane was ever found.[1]

2. Knute Rockne, football coach (1888–1931)
Rockne was riding on a Transcontinental Western NC-999 from Kansas City to Los Angeles. The cause of the crash, in a pasture thirty-four miles west of Emporia, was never accurately determined. According to several farmers who saw the crash, a wing snapped off the plane (apparently due to ice), and sent it plummeting into the field. There was no explosion or fire, but all eight people on board were killed on impact.[2]

3. Will Rogers, American humorist (1879–1935), and Wiley Post, aviator (1898–1935)
Post's plane was a modified Lockheed Orion with a Pratt & Whitney Wasp engine. On an Alaskan sightseeing trip, the two defied a forecast of zero-visibility weather to continue their trip

48   THE BOOK OF LOSERS

from Fairbanks to Barrow on August 15, 1935. The forecast was accurate; Post became somewhat lost and put the plane down on desolate Walakpa Lagoon to ask some Eskimos (whom he had seen from the air) for directions. Upon receiving some directions, Post then lifted the plane off the lagoon. However, as it started to climb, the engine sputtered and went dead. The plane crashed headlong into the sand, splitting the fuselage open, and killing the two instantly.[3]

4. Carole Lombard, American actress (1908–1942)

Lombard took off from Las Vegas in a TWA plane at 7:07 P.M. January 16, 1942, for Los Angeles, where she was to meet her husband, Clark Gable, after a war-bonds tour. Thirty minutes later, an explosion and flare were heard and seen near Table Mountain, about thirty miles southwest of Las Vegas. The rescuers were hampered by heavy snow and rugged terrain at an elevation of 8100 feet. When they found the wreckage, bodies were terribly burned and strewn for hundreds of yards around the mountain peak; Miss Lombard's body was not immediately recognizable. Later it was learned that she had originally wanted to take a train to Los Angeles, but had agreed to a coin flip with her agent, who wanted to fly. Tails won, and they flew.[4]

5. Joseph P. Kennedy, Jr. (1915–1944)

Kennedy took off in his Liberator B-24 bomber "Zoot-Zoot-Black" from an airfield near Diss, England, on August 12, 1944, to destroy a German rocket-launching pad on the French coast. The plane carried ten tons of explosives, and the plan called for Kennedy and his copilot to set the plane on a remote control course for the target, then bail out. At 6:20 P.M. at 15,000 feet, they homed in the airplane's radio on the rocket site, and Kennedy threw the remote control switch. The detonation device malfunctioned and the plane exploded in a ball of fire which

LOSERS OF LIFE 49

could be seen for miles; Kennedy and his copilot were killed instantly.[5]

6. Glenn Miller, American bandleader (1904–1944)

Miller left England on December 15, 1944, in a nine-seater C-64 Norseman for a flight to Paris. The weather was miserable, but the single-engine plane had no de-icing equipment, nor could it float. The plane never arrived at its destination. Rescue attempts were greatly hampered by the fact that no radio communication was allowed; the Battle of the Bulge was about to begin. To this day, no one knows what happened.[6]

7. Buddy Holly, Ritchie Valens, J.P. (The Big Bopper) Richardson, American pop singers

The singers, while making a tour of midwestern cities, chartered a Bonanza four-seater single-engine plane to take them to Fargo, North Dakota, on the night of February 4, 1959. The plane crashed shortly after takeoff from Clear Lake, Iowa, at about 2:00 A.M. in a snowy farm field. It skidded for 558 feet, throwing Holly and Valens twenty feet from the plane, and Richardson forty feet away; all died instantly. The three were accustomed to traveling by bus, but on this occasion had hoped to arrive in Fargo early, so they could do their laundry before their next concert.[7]

8. Dag Hammarskjold, U.N. Secretary-General (1905–1961)

The secretary-general's plane, the DC-68 "Albertina," crashed just before landing at Ndola, a city in northern Rhodesia (Zambia) on September 7, 1961. The landing appeared to be proceeding normally when the plane dipped into a forest, its propellers cutting the treetops. After plowing through 800 feet of forest, what remained of the left wing hit the base of an anthill, swinging the aircraft around and igniting it. Thrown clear of the

50   THE BOOK OF LOSERS

flames, Hammarskjold probably survived the crash but died of internal injuries before rescuers could reach him. [8]

9. Rocky Marciano, American heavyweight boxer (1924–1969)

Marciano's small single-engine plane crashed en route from Des Moines to Chicago near the central Iowa town of Jasper, one day before his 46th birthday on September 1, 1969. The plane was making its landing approach when it slammed into a wooded area at approximately 10 P.M. E.D.T. All the passengers died instantly. [9]

10. Lin Piao, Chinese defense minister

According to Chinese reports, Lin died when the Trident jet in which he was flying crashed northeast of the Mongolian capital of Ulan Bator on July 29, 1971. At the time of the crash, Lin was defense minister of China as well as vice chairman of the Chinese Communist Party. Government sources claimed that he had just attempted to assassinate Chairman Mao, and was fleeing to the Soviet Union when the crash occurred. [10]

11. Hale Boggs, American congressman

On October 16, 1972, the twin-engine, white-and-orange Cessna 310 that was carrying the House Majority Leader disappeared during a rainstorm, in a rugged mountain wilderness along the Gulf of Alaska. The plane's route from Anchorage took it over the Chugach Mountains, along the Alaskan coast to Glacier National Monument on its way to Juneau. Despite an intensive search, no plane wreckage was found. [11]

12. Mrs. E. Howard Hunt

The Boeing 737's approach to Midway Airport (Illinois) on December 8, 1972, was too high and too fast, so an air traffic controller ordered the pilot to circle the field. When the pilot

LOSERS OF LIFE

attempted to comply, the plane went into a stall. Instead of pointing the nose of the plane down while applying power, the United Airlines pilot apparently pointed it up. The plane then plummeted to the ground, killing Mrs. Hunt and forty-three other people. Later stories suggested the plane had been sabotaged; investigators found $10,000 in her purse, all the more curious because of her reputed role as funneler of money throughout the Watergate era. Nonetheless, the family claimed the money was a down payment for the initial franchise fee of a Holiday Inn.[12]

13. Roberto Clemente, baseball player (1934–1973)

Clemente's four-engine DC-7, loaded with relief supplies for the survivors of the Nicaraguan earthquake, took off from San Juan, Puerto Rico, on January 1, 1973. It went down over the ocean approximately one and a half hours later at 9:22 P.M.; U.S. Coast Guard boats found only bits of wreckage and no survivors. Clemente's plane had been delayed for over five hours, and he told his wife shortly before leaving: "If there's one more thing, we're going to leave it until tomorrow." The cause of the crash was unknown.[13]

14. Jim Croce, pop singer (1943–1973)

Croce had just completed a concert at Northwestern Louisiana University on September 22, 1973, and was headed for his next engagement at Sherman, Texas, when his plan crashed on takeoff. The exact cause was undetermined, but the twin-engine Beechcraft D-18 struck a 30-foot-high tree 250 feet beyond the runway. Croce and his five companions died instantly.[14]

15. Dolly Sinatra

The Learjet in which Mrs. Sinatra was riding crashed into the side of San Gorgonio Mountain in southern California on

52   THE BOOK OF LOSERS

January 6, 1977. The plane was en route to Las Vegas, where she was going to see her son Frank's opening at Caesar's Palace. The blame for the crash was apparently pinned on the Palm Springs control tower; more specifically, the Palm Springs airport lacked necessary radar equipment because of a desert beautification project.[15]

16. Audie Murphy, American war hero (1925–1971)

Murphy's small chartered plane crashed on Brushy Mountain in Virginia on a business trip from Atlanta to Martinsville, Virginia. The pilot of the plane overflew the small Martinsville airport during a thunderstorm. Murphy was trapped in the flaming wreckage and apparently died on impact or shortly afterward. Ironically, the crash took place on the last Monday in May (the 31st)—Memorial Day.[16]

PRIMARY SOURCES (Mainly from multiple newspaper accounts):
1. *Encyclopedia Americana*, 1976, vol. 1.
2. *New York Times*, April 1, 1931.
3. Richard Ketchum, *Will Rogers: His Life and Times*. New York: American Heritage, 1973.
4. *Los Angeles Times*, January 17, 1942.
5. Primary Source: Rose Kennedy, *Times to Remember*. New York: Doubleday & Co., 1974.
6. George Simon, *Glenn Miller and His Orchestra*. New York: Thomas Crowell, 1974.
7. *New York Times*, Feb. 4, 1959.
8. Arthur Gavshon, *The Mysterious Death of Dag Hammarskjold*. New York: Walker & Co., 1962.
9. *New York Times*, Sept. 1, 1969.
10. *Time*, October 23, 1972.
11. *Los Angeles Times*, Nov. 25, 1972.
12. *New York Times*, Dec. 10, 1972.
13. *New York Times*, Jan. 2, 1973.
14. *Los Angeles Times*, Sept. 22, 1973.
15. *Los Angeles Times*, Jan. 11, 1977.
16. *New York Times*, June 1, 1971.

STATES IN WHICH YOU ARE MOST LIKELY TO ACCIDENTALLY BURN TO DEATH (1970)

(rate per 100,000 population in resident state)

Alaska	10.3
District of Columbia	7.5
Mississippi	7.2
South Carolina	6.6
New Mexico	5.8
Alabama	5.8
Georgia	5.6
North Carolina	4.8
Oklahoma	4.7
Louisiana	4.7
Tennessee	4.7

Source: Statistical Bureau of the Metropolitan Life Insurance Company.

TEN WORST LOSSES OF LIFE DUE TO FIRES (NATURAL, MANMADE, EXPLOSION, FOREST)

1. 38,000: Tokyo–Yokohama, Japan, Sept. 1, 1923

A fire burned through the cities following a large earthquake, 40,000 people sought safety in an open area near the Sumida River. The fire turned and swept over the area; most of the people died while still standing packed together.

54 THE BOOK OF LOSERS

2. 7,000: Constantinople, Turkey, 1729
A fire raged through most of the city.

3. 4,000: Isle of Rhodes, Greece, 1856
The Ottoman Turks were using a church on the island as their ammunition depot. The church was struck by lightning, igniting the gunpowder, causing a tremendous explosion and fire.

4. 3,000: Brescia, Italy, 1769
Over 100 tons of the city's gunpowder exploded, destroying a sixth of the city.

5. 1,700: Chunking, China, September 2, 1949
Details are scarce, but a fire roared through the riverfront area with disastrous results.

6. 1,600: Halifax, Nova Scotia, December 6, 1917
The French munitions ship *Mont Blanc,* carrying 450,000 tons of TNT, 23,000 tons of picric acid, and 35 tons of benzol, was hit broadside by the freighter *Imo.* The French abandoned ship rather than fight the fire, which resulted in an explosion that destroyed 300 acres of the city.

7. 1,600: Canton, China, May 1845
Though firm documentation is missing, the high death toll apparently resulted from a fire which swept through a popular theater.

8. 1,549: Honkeiko, Manchuria, April 26, 1942
An explosion in the Honkeiko colliery was responsible for these deaths.

LOSERS OF LIFE

9. 1,500: Peshtigo, Wisconsin, October 8, 1871

On this night, the drought-stricken forest town was engulfed in a fire-storm; a blast of hot air shot through the buildings. Everything was set on fire, including 1,300 residents. The fire continued through the forests of northern Wisconsin, burning another 200 people to death. It was the worst fire in U.S. history, but went largely unreported because it occurred on the same day, and at almost the same hour, as the Great Chicago Fire (in which only 200 died).

10. 1,450: Mississippi River, April 27, 1865

An old paddle-wheeler, the *Sultana*, was being used to return Union soldiers home at the close of the Civil War. Around 2 A.M., the Sultana's number-3 boiler exploded. Hundreds of soldiers were trapped in the ensuing flames, and since no accurate records were kept of who was on the boat, many families never knew the real fate of their men. The largest maritime disaster in U.S. history received little publicity; on April 26, the Confederacy had surrendered and John Wilkes Booth had been shot.

Primary Source: James Cornell, *The Great International Disaster Book*. New York: Charles Scribner's Sons, 1976.

Twelve States in Which You Are Most Likely to Lose Your Life by Accidentally Drowning (1970)

(Rate per 100,000 population by state of residence)

Alaska	8.6
Florida	6.8
Nevada	5.9
Louisiana	5.7
South Carolina	5.2
Mississippi	5.1
Idaho	5.0
Arkansas	4.8
Arizona	4.8
Delaware	4.5
Montana	4.5
New Mexico	4.5

Source: Statistical Bureau of the Metropolitan Life Insurance Company.

Worst Instances of Mass Loss of Life by Drowning

Lives Lost*	Date/Location/Events
900,000–6,000,000	September–October 1887: The Yellow River flooded 11 cities and 300 villages, covering 50,000 square miles to depths of twenty to thirty feet.

* Estimation

LOSERS OF LIFE

57

500,000	1939: Due to wartime conditions, no exact information exists concerning this series of floods, which occurred in northern China.
500,000–1,000,000	November 13, 1970: A cyclone struck East Pakistan, carrying 100-mph winds and seas fifteen feet above normal. Over 1.1 million acres of rice paddies disappeared along with all their human inhabitants.
300,000	October 7, 1737: Forty-foot waves, spurred by high cyclone winds, engulfed the land at the mouth of the Hooghly River near Calcutta, India.
300,000	1881: Most of the victims drowned immediately following a cyclone which struck Haiphong, Vietnam. Tremendous tidal waves swamped the area at the mouth of the Red River on the Gulf of Tonkin.
300,000	April 23, 1969: Again, due to a blackout in China, no exact figures were reported when Shantung Province was covered with water. The figure is the estimate of Japanese newsmen.
300,000	1642: At least this many people drowned when rebels destroyed the dikes at Kaifeng, China, flooding the city and surrounding area.
100,000	1876: A tropical cyclone struck the Bay of Bengal, sweeping twenty-foot waves down on the offshore islands near Bengal, India.
100,000	June 6, 1882: A cyclone from the Arabian Sea drove high waves into Bombay, India.

THE BOOK OF LOSERS

100,000	1099: Storm waves flooded areas of coastal England and the Netherlands.
100,000	1228: Friesland in the Netherlands was swamped by high waves.
100,000	1911: China's Yangtze River overflowed its banks after heavy rains.

Primary Source: James Cornell, *The Great International Disaster Book*. New York: Charles Scribner's Sons, 1976.

FAMOUS PEOPLE WHO LOST THEIR LIVES BY FIRE OR WATER

Lord, Lord! me thought, what pain it was to drown:
What dreadful noise of waters in mine ears!
What ugly sights of death within mine eyes!
SHAKESPEARE, *Richard III*

1. Percy Bysshe Shelley, English poet (1792–1822)

Shelley ventured out on his boat *Ariel* between two and three o'clock in the afternoon; a storm coming in from the Italian Gulf quickly obscured the *Ariel*. Twenty minutes later the storm passed, but Shelley's boat had vanished. Five days later, after an extensive search, Shelley's horribly bloated body washed ashore near Via Reggio. Fish had eaten his face, hands, and other unprotected body parts, but he was identifiable by possessions in his clothes.[1]

LOSERS OF LIFE

59

2. Buck Jones, American western-movie actor (1894–1942)

The actor died in the famous Coconut Grove fire in Boston on the night of November 28, 1942. The fire started when a busboy lit a match so that he could see to replace a light socket, and accidentally set fire to an artificial palm tree. In addition to Jones, 490 people perished in the smoke and flames.[2]

3. Zelda Fitzgerald (1901–1948)

Zelda had been confined to Highland's Mental Hospital in Asheville, North Carolina. At about midnight on March 10, 1948, the hospital kitchen erupted in fire. Most of the patients were asleep; rescue attempts were thwarted by the barred doors and windows. Firemen were able to save women on the first and second floors, but nine others, including Zelda, died on the third floor. The heat of the fire completely immolated the women; Zelda could not be identified.[3]

4. Linda Darnell, American actress (1921–1965)

Ms. Darnell was visiting a friend's Chicago town house when fire broke out in the living room area. Apparently she became confused and trapped; when firemen found her near the sofa, burns covered 80 percent of her body. She was taken to the burn treatment center of Cook County Hospital, where she died at 2:25 P.M. on April 11, 1965.[6]

5. Harold E. Holt, Prime Minister of Australia (1908–1967)

The Australian leader drowned while skin-diving on December, 7, 1967, near his home at Portsea, Australia—outside Melbourne. Holt entered the ocean at approximately 1:40 P.M., searching for crayfish; his swimming companion became alarmed when he did not surface after a long period under water.[4]

60   THE BOOK OF LOSERS

6. Richard Tregaskis, American journalist and author (1916–1973)

The six-foot-seven-inch writer drowned on August 17, 1973, while swimming in the ocean near Honolulu; later, doctors speculated that he may have suffered a heart attack in the surf.[5]

7. Joe Flynn, American actor (1925–1974)

Flynn accidentally drowned in his Bel-Air swimming pool on the night of July 19, 1974. His nude body was not found until 7:30 A.M. the next morning by his wife and daughter, who pulled him from the pool. Attempts to revive him were futile.[7]

8. Jack Cassidy, American actor (1927–1976)

The actor's living quarters were destroyed by a blaze on December 12, 1976, that swept through his penthouse apartment. Cassidy's body was so badly burned that normal identification was impossible; dental records were located to establish identity. Police theorized that he may have been smoking in bed.[8]

9. Virgil (Gus) Grissom (1926–1967), Edward H. White (1930–1967), Roger Chaffee (1936–1967); U.S. astronauts

These three Apollo astronauts were killed in a flash fire which enveloped their Apollo craft at 6:15 P.M. on January 28, 1967. During routine checkout simulation exercises at Cape Kennedy, flames erupted after an unexplained spark ignited in the pure oxygen of the pressurized cabin. Intense heat prevented rescuers from reaching the capsule, which was atop the service tower, for ten to fifteen minutes. By this time, only the charred bodies of the astronauts remained.[9]

10. Carroll Rosenbloom, sports entrepreneur (1907–1979)

On Monday, April 2, 1979, Rosenbloom was swimming in rough seas off Golden Beach, Florida. He was apparently

LOSERS OF LIFE

dragged out to sea by a strong undertow, and he drowned despite the efforts of rescuers.[10]

SOURCES:
1. Andre, Maurois, *Ariel: the Life of Shelley*. New York: Ungar, 1968 ed.
2. *New York Times*, Dec. 1, 1942.
3. Sara Mayfield, *Exiles from Paradise: Zelda and Scott Fitzgerald*. New York: Delacourt, 1971.
4. *New York Times*, April 11, 1965.
5. *New York Times*, Dec. 17, 1967.
6. *Los Angeles Times*, Aug. 17, 1973.
7. *Los Angeles Times*, July 20, 1974.
8. *Los Angeles Times*, Dec. 13, 1976.
9. *New York Times*, Jan. 28, 1967.
10. *Los Angeles Times*, April 3, 1979.

TEN STATES IN WHICH YOU ARE MOST LIKELY TO FALL TO YOUR DEATH (1970)

(Rate per 100,000 population by state of residence)

Massachusetts	13.1
Nebraska	11.9
District of Columbia	11.8
Montana	11.2
Missouri	11.1
Ohio	10.9
Maine	10.7
Kentucky	10.5
Rhode Island	10.0
Kansas	10.0

Source of raw data: Statistical Bureau of the Metropolitan Life Insurance Company.

62   *THE BOOK OF LOSERS*

TEN GREATEST LOSSES OF LIFE CAUSED BY FALLING MATTER OR PEOPLE FALLING (EARTHQUAKES)

Date	Location	Lives Lost *
January 24, 1556	Shensi Province, China	830,000
July 28, 1976	Tangshan, China	655,000
October 11, 1737	Calcutta, India	300,000
December 16, 1920	Kansu Province, China	200,000
September 1, 1923	Tokyo-Yokohama, Japan	140,000
September 27, 1290	Gulf of Chihli, China	100,000
1731	Peking, China	100,000
1693	Naples, Italy	93,000
December 28, 1908	Messina, Italy	75–85,000
November 1667	Shemakha, Caucasia	80,000

* Estimated on basis of available evidence.

LOSERS OF LIFE 63

PEOPLE WHO FELL TO THEIR DEATHS

He that is down can fall no lower.
SAMUEL BUTLER, *Hudibras*

1. George Bernard Shaw, Irish dramatist (1856–1950)

On September 10, 1950, Shaw was trimming trees and shrubs in his garden when he fell and broke his hip. He underwent two successful operations the next day and seemed on the way to recovery. However, the fall aroused a long-dormant kidney infection which killed him a month later.[1]

2. Amy Vanderbilt, journalist (1908–1974)

The syndicated etiquette columnist fell to her death in the early evening of December 27, 1974, from a second-story window of her town house on New York's East 87th Street. Death came as a result of severe head injuries and was instantaneous; passersby discovered her on the concrete near the door of her house.[2]

3. A.J. Bakunas, stunt man (1951–1978)

In an attempt to set a world-record 323-foot free fall in Lexington, Kentucky, Bakunas was killed September 22, 1978, when the air bag he designed burst when he hit it at 115 mph. He broke both hips and shoulderblades, but the fatal injury was a pulmonary contusion.[3]

4. Dieter Schepp, East German aerialist(?–1962)

On the night of January 30, 1962, the Wallenda family was performing its complicated pyramid (seven people in three tiers)

64   THE BOOK OF LOSERS

high-wire act in Detroit. Schepp, Karl Wallenda's nephew, was
making his first appearance in the group when he lost his grip,
screaming: "I can't hold on anymore!" The entire pyramid
collapsed; Schepp died instantly on the concrete floor below.[4]

5. Henrietta Wallenda, German aerialist (1921–1963)

On the night of April 18, 1963, the finale of Ms. Wallenda's
act called for her to sway in a wide arc while standing on top of a
fifty-foot fiberglass pole (she was using a substitute pole after her
usual one had broken in her previous performance). She seemed
to be performing normally, when the pole suddenly snapped
backward, sending her plunging downward. Her impact was
somewhat lessened by a guy wire ten feet from the Omaha
auditorium floor, but she died instantly of a broken neck.[5]

6. Richard Guzman, German aerialist (1941–1972)

The son-in-law of Karl Wallenda was performing with the
family when he inadvertently touched a live electrical wire while
climbing a pole to start his act. The shock knocked him off the
pole and sent him reeling sixty feet to the ground. Though his
breathing was restored after intense mouth-to-mouth respiration,
he died shortly afterward at a Wheeling, West Virginia, hospital
on July 29, 1972.[6]

7. Karl Wallenda, German aerialist (1905–1978)

Wallenda was walking across a 300-foot wire strung between
two beachfront hotels in San Juan, Puerto Rico, when a gust of
wind suddenly shook the wire. He crouched down to no avail;
another gust hit him, and he plummeted 100 feet to instantaneous death, landing on the roof of a taxi, then bouncing
off onto the sidewalk.[4]

LOSERS OF LIFE 65

SOURCES:
1. Archibald Henderson, *George Bernard Shaw: Man of the Century*. New York: Appleton-Century-Crofts, 1956.
2. *New York Times*, Dec. 28, 1974.
3. *San Francisco Chronicle*, Sept. 23, 1978.
4. *Time*, April 3, 1978.
5. *New York Times*, April 19, 1963.
6. *New York Times*, July 29, 1972.

TEN DISEASES TO WHICH YOU ARE MOST LIKELY TO LOSE YOUR LIFE

Heart disease
Malignant neoplasms (cancerous tumors)
Cerebrovascular disease (apoplexy or stroke)
Enteritis (and other diarrheal diseases)
Influenza and Pneumonia
Bronchitis, Emphysema, and Asthma
Diabetes mellitus
Cirrhosis of the liver
Tuberculosis
Diseases at birth

Source: David Wallechinsky, Irving Wallace, and Amy Wallace, *The Book of Lists*. New York: Bantam, 1977.

STATES IN WHICH YOU ARE MOST LIKELY TO LOSE YOUR LIFE BY NATURAL OR ACCIDENTAL CAUSES (PER 1000 IN POPULATION) (1975–76)

West Virginia	10.8
District of Columbia	10.4
Florida	10.4
Missouri	10.3
Arkansas	10.3
Pennsylvania	10.2
Oklahoma	10.0
Iowa	9.8
Kentucky	9.8
Maine	9.7
Mississippi	9.7

Source of raw data: National Center for Health Statistics

COUNTRIES WHOSE INHABITANTS ARE LIKELY TO LOSE THEIR LIVES BEFORE AGE 39

Men	Life Expectancy At Birth
Gabon	25.0
Chad	29.0
Togo	31.6
Upper Volta	32.1
Central African Empire	33.0
West Cameroon	34.3
Bangladesh	35.8
Mali	36.5
Ethiopia	36.5
Angola	37.0
Mauritania	37.0
Guinea-Bissau	37.0

Women	
Upper Volta	31.1
Chad	35.0
Bangladesh	35.8
Central African Empire	36.0
Nigeria	36.7
Ghana	37.08
West Cameroon	37.2
Benin	37.3
Madagascar	38.3
Togo	38.5

Source: *United Nations Demographic Yearbook,* 1977.

–III–

Political Losers

TWENTY PEOPLE WHO LOST THEIR COUNTRIES

What greater grief than the loss of one's native land?
EURIPIDES, *Medea*

1. Sinuhe, Egyptian citizen, (c. 2000 B.C.)

According to sketchy hieroglyphics, the world's first recorded exile was booted out of Egypt for a political indiscretion. Still a young man, Sinuhe resolved to make the best of his lot, traveled about most of the known world, and raised a family. However, by the time that his sons had "grown beards" the old man began to long again for his home on the Nile. He sent a letter to the reigning pharaoh, Sesostris I, recanting his past misdeeds and begging permission to return to his country. He was granted a pardon, and died in the service of his pharaoh.

2. Themistocles, Greek soldier (banished 471 B.C.)

In 480 B.C. Themistocles was the toast of the Greek nation, having commanded the victorious Greek fleet in their battle with the troops of Xerxes at Salamis. However, his fame soured quickly; a short nine years later he was convicted of embezzlement and exiled. For five years he traveled from court to court, finally making his way to Persia and the court of Xerxes. There,

POLITICAL LOSERS

69

intent on revenge, he lived in honor and respect; unfortunately, he died before he could satiate his vengeance.

3. Hyperbolus, Greek bureaucrat (exiled 417 B.C.)

This low-born Athenian was the last person obstracized from Athens. Sick of a quarrel between Alcibiades and Nicias, he maneuvered the members of the banishment committee into voting to banish one or the other. However, just before the vote was to be taken, Alcibiades and Nicias patched up their argument. Rather than waste all the preparations that had been made, the committee went ahead with a vote and decided to banish Hyperbolus instead.

4. Euripides, Greek playwright (c. 480–406 B.C.)

His speculation in *Medea* notwithstanding, Euripides decided at age seventy-one that the loss of his country was better than the constant harping of the comedy writers and certain domestic troubles he had. Though his exile was voluntary, he remained an expatriate until his death.

5. Aristotle, Greek philosopher, scientist, critic (384–322 B.C.)

Late in life, Aristotle found himself accused of impiety, and feared for his life. "In order to save the Athenians a second time sinning against philosophy," Aristotle fled to Chalcis. He died there a year later, an apparent suicide.

6. Publius Ovidius Naso (Ovid), Roman poet (43 B.C.–17 A.D.)

Ovid had the misfortune to be implicated in the adulterous scandal which erupted about Augustus Caesar's daughter, Julia (also exiled). The angry emperor deported Ovid, without trial, to a lonely spot on the Black Sea called Tomi. There he lived for the remainder of his life, never being allowed to return to Rome.

70 THE BOOK OF LOSERS

His stint in exile fortunately did not dull his creative mind. He mastered the language of the area, and wrote his final poems in it.

7. Muhammad, founder of Islam (570–632)

Islam has its beginnings in the prophet's exile from Mecca in A.D. 622, and his subsequent flight (Hegira) to Medina. Some eight years later he led 10,000 of his followers against Mecca; the city surrendered, and Muhammad became chief and prophet.

8. Dante Alighieri, Italian poet (1265–1321)

For refusing to obey the orders of Pope Boniface VIII, Dante (who was in Rome at the time) was ordered exiled from Florence, and faced the pleasant sentence of being burned alive if captured. For the next nineteen years he journeyed through Europe, visiting Paris and other points of cultural interest. But whatever he did, his thoughts were always on his beloved city. On occasion he attempted to devise ways to enter Florence, but was always rebuffed. He died in Ravenna, one of the most famous exiles in history.

9. Niccolò Machiavelli, Italian political theorist (1469–1527)

Machiavelli's staunch support of republican sentiments led to his torture and exile from Florence. Rather than being deported to another country, he was confined to his small estate near San Casciano for sixteen years. While there he wrote *The Prince*, and eventually worked himself back into the Medicis' favor. However, just when life was looking rosy again, the Medicis were deposed by the republicans. Machiavelli was accused of betraying his principles to gain favor, and was forced to continue in exile.

10. François Marie Arouet de Voltaire, French philosopher (1694–1778)

Voltaire had the dubious distinction to endure two exiles. The

POLITICAL LOSERS 71

first occurred after an argument with the powerful Rohan family and sent him first to the Bastille and then to England, where he remained for three years before obtaining approval to return to Paris in 1729. In 1751, Voltaire decided to visit Frederick II of Prussia and remained there for three creative years; upon returning, he discovered that he had been banished from Paris. He moved to a home just outside of Geneva; from this vantage point, he became the literary and cultural center of Europe. He finally was able to return to Paris in 1778, where he died two months later.

11. Germaine de Staël, French courtesan and intellectual (1766–1817)

Termed by many historians as the "first modern woman" and the greatest female French writer, Germaine had the audacity to work for Napoleon's deposal right under his nose, in her Parisian salon. Finally her actions became too threatening to ignore, and she was banished from Paris in 1802. She did have the last laugh, however, returning to Paris after the overthrow of the Third Empire in 1814, and Napoleon's subsequent exile.

12. Napoleon Bonaparte, French political and military leader (1769–1821)

Following his defeat at Waterloo, Napoleon was sent to the island of Elba. From this point, he organized another challenge to the French government and reentered France for the famous 100 days. Defeated again, he lived out the remainder of his life in exile on the island of St. Helena.

13. Victor Hugo, French writer (1802–1885)

In 1851, Hugo organized the republican opposition to Louis Napoleon, and was promptly exiled when his forces were defeated. A few years later, from his exile in Jersey, he sent a treasonous note to Louis challenging him to expel him again.

72   THE BOOK OF LOSERS

The Jersey authorities were not amused and banished him; he then fled to Guernsey, where he lived for fifteen years, writing such works as *Les Miserables*. When France became a republic once again in 1870, Hugo returned to Paris in glory.

14. Karl Marx, German philosopher (1818–1883)

Six months after the 1848 French Revolution, Marx and Friedrich Engels were in Cologne, Germany, editing a newspaper called the *Organ of Democracy*. The German king proceeded to dissolve the national government, whereupon Marx and Engels advocated nonpayment of taxes and organized military resistance to the king. Arrested, Marx was tried for high treason, but was unanimously acquitted by a middle-class jury. Following the verdict, the king banished him from Germany, and he spent his remaining thirty-four years in London. It was there at the British Museum that he wrote *Das Kapital*.

15–18. Sigmund Freud (1856–1939), Thomas Mann (1875–1955, Albert Einstein (1879–1955), Bertolt Brecht (1898–1956)

These men were just four of the countless thousands of Jewish intellectuals who were exiled from their native countries by the Nazi occupation of Europe. Freud died an exile in London; Mann was the only exile to return to Europe and be celebrated by both East and West Germany; Einstein remained an exile, moving permanently to the U.S.; Brecht returned to East Germany and won the Stalin Peace Prize in 1954.

19. Leon Trotsky, Russian revolutionary (1879–1940)

When Lenin died, Trotsky's attempt to take power was thwarted by Stalin. He was expelled from the U.S.S.R. in February 1929, first living in Turkey and then France. Stalin's agents were always close behind, however; he was soon forced to live in Norway, then Mexico. Meanwhile, in the Soviet Union,

POLITICAL LOSERS

73

he had become the object of a government campaign which depicted him as the leader of a vast anti-Soviet plot. His followers were executed after the Moscow Trials (1936–38), and Trotsky was assassinated with an axe in 1940, after eleven years in exile.

20. Alexandr Solzhenitsyn, Russian novelist and historian (1918–)

The Russian writer was arrested again in 1974 for his disparaging writing about the Soviet government, but in a surprise move Soviet authorities proceeded to deprive him of his citizenship and deport him. He moved first to Switzerland and later to the U.S., where he lives in permanent exile.

Primary source of raw data: Paul Tabori, *The Anatomy of Exile: A Semantic and Historical Study.* London: Harrap, 1972.

BLACKLIST LOSERS

---

*Reputation, reputation, reputation! O! I have lost
my reputation, I have lost the immortal part of myself,
and what remains is bestial.*

SHAKESPEARE, *Othello*

In 1950, *Counterattack* magazine issued *Red Channels*, which listed all those entertainment people suspected of having Communist sympathies. The *Red Channels* list was the basis of the infamous Hollywood blacklist, and resulted in many of the following losing all employment for a time, and others losing particular jobs. *Counterattack* editors usually listed a number of Communist "connections" for each person; in a few instances, people had already acknowledged Communist Party membership.

74   *THE BOOK OF LOSERS*

[Selected] Persons	*[Selected] Basis of "Communist" Allegation*
Leonard Bernstein *Composer/Conductor*	American-Soviet Music Society
Lee J. Cobb *Actor*	National Council of the Arts, Sciences and Professions
Aaron Copland *Composer*	Scientific and Cultural Conference for World Peace
Howard Da Silva *Actor*	Actor's Laboratory Theater
Howard Duff *Actor*	Committee for the First Amendment
José Ferrer *Actor*	Joint Anti-Fascist Refugee Committee
Will Geer *Actor*	Married to Herta Ware, granddaughter of Ella Reeve Bloor, veteran Communist leader
Ruth Gordon *Actress*	Progressive Citizens of America
Dashiell Hammett *Author*	League of American Writers
Lillian Hellman *Playwright*	National Council of American-Soviet Friendship
Judy Holliday *Actress*	Stop Censorship Committee
Lena Horne *Actress*	Council on African Affairs
Langston Hughes *Poet*	Friends of the Abraham Lincoln Brigade

POLITICAL LOSERS

Burl Ives *Actor*	Southern Conference for Human Welfare
Sam Jaffe *Actor*	End Jim Crow in Baseball Committee
Garson Kanin *Playwright*	American Youth for Democracy
Gypsy Rose Lee *Singer*	Hollywood Anti-Nazi League
Burgess Meredith *Actor*	American Committee for Yugoslav Relief
Arthur Miller *Playwright*	Book Find Club
Henry Morgan *Actor*	Veterans Against Discrimination of Civil Rights Congress
Zero Mostel *Actor*	Civil Rights Congress
Edward G. Robinson *Actor*	Hollywood Democratic Committee
Pete Seeger *Folksinger*	Jefferson School of Social Science
Artie Shaw *Bandleader*	National Negro Congress
Howard K. Smith *Newscaster*	For various statements on radio
Gale Sondergaard *Actress*	American Continental Congress for Peace
Orson Welles *Actor/Director*	Theater Arts Committee

76 THE BOOK OF LOSERS

58 LOSERS OF U.S. PRESIDENTIAL NOMINATION

(All of the following received at least one vote in favor of their nomination, but some were not formally nominated)
Democrats

1. Edmund G. Brown, Jr. (1976)
2. Edmund G. Brown, Sr. (1956)
3. William Jennings Bryan (1912)
4. Harry F. Byrd (1932)
5. James Buchanan (1844, 1848, 1852)
6. John C. Calhoun (1844, 1852)
7. Shirley Chisholm (1972)
8. Jefferson Davis (1860)
9. Stephen Douglas (1952)
10. J. William Fulbright (1952)
11. John Nance Garner (1932, 1940)
12. Averell Harriman (1952, 1956)
13. William Randolph Hearst (1904, 1920)
14. Sam Houston (1852)
15. Cordell Hull (1924, 1928, 1940)
16. Hubert Humphrey (1972)
17. Henry Jackson (1972, 1976)
18. Andrew Johnson (1860, 1868)
19. Lyndon Johnson (1956, 1960)
20. Edward Kennedy (1968)
21. Eugene McCarthy (1968)
22. George McGovern (1968)
23. Edmund Muskie (1972)
24. John J. Pershing (1920)
25. Will Rogers (1932)
26. Franklin Roosevelt (1924)
27. Al Smith (1920, 1924)

POLITICAL LOSERS

28. Adlai Stevenson (1892, 1896)
29. George Wallace (1972)

Republicans

1. Cassius Clay (1860)
2. Calvin Coolidge (1920, 1928)
3. Thomas Dewey (1940)
5. Frederick Douglass (1888)
5. Coleman du Pont (1920)
6. Millard Fillmore (1848)
7. John C. Fremont (1860)
8. Barry Goldwater (1960)
9. Ulysses S. Grant (1880)
10. Rutherford B. Hayes (1880)
11. Warren Harding (1916)
12. Herbert Hoover (1920, 1949)
13. Charles Evans Hughes (1908)
14. Robert La Follette (1908, 1924)
15. Fiorello La Guardia (1940)
16. Henry Cabot Lodge (1964)
17. Douglas MacArthur (1944, 1948, 1952)
18. William McKinley (1888, 1892)
19. Ronald Reagan (1968, 1976)
20. Nelson Rockefeller (1964, 1968)
21. Winthrop Rockefeller (1968)
22. George Romney (1964, 1968)
23. Theodore Roosevelt (1908, 1916)
24. William Seward (1860)
25. John Sherman (1884)
26. William T. Sherman (1884)
27. Harold Stassen (1952, 1968)
28. William Howard Taft (1916)
29. Earl Warren (1948, 1952)

Source: Richard C. Bain and Judith H. Parris, *Convention Decisions and Voting Records*, Washington: The Brookings Institution, 1973.

LOSERS OF U.S. PRESIDENTIAL ELECTIONS

	Year	Loser (2nd place)	Electoral Vote Margin	Popular Vote Margin
1.	1796	Thomas Jefferson	3	Unknown
2.	1800	Aaron Burr	0: Lost by vote of House of Representatives due to tie.	Unknown
3.	1804	Charles Pinckney	148	Unknown
4.	1808	Charles Pinckney	75	Unknown
5.	1812	DeWitt Clinton	39	Unknown
6.	1816	Rufus King	139	Unknown
7.	1820	John Quincy Adams	230	Unknown
8.	1824	Andrew Jackson	Jackson had 15 more electoral votes. Lost by vote of House. Had no majority.	Jackson had 50,511 more votes
9.	1828	John Quincy Adams	95	138,134
10.	1832	Henry Clay	170	157,313
11.	1836	William H. Harrison	97	214,671
12.	1840	Martin Van Buren	174	146,315
13.	1844	Henry Clay	65	38,185
14.	1848	Lewis Cass	36	149,557
15.	1852	Winfield Scott	212	214,896
16.	1856	John C. Fremont	60	536,440

POLITICAL LOSERS

79

17.	1860	Stephen Douglas	168	491,195
		John Breckinridge	108	1,020,589
18.	1864	George McClellan	191	407,342
19.	1868	Horatio Seymour	134	305,456
20.	1872	Horace Greeley	Died before vote	762,991
21.	1876	Samuel Tilden	1	Tilden had 250,807 more votes
22.	1880	Winfield Hancock	59	7,023
23.	1884	James G. Blaine	37	62,683
24.	1888	Grover Cleveland	65	Cleveland had 95,713 more votes
25.	1892	Benjamin Harrison	132	363,612
26.	1896	William Jennings Bryan	95	567,692
27.	1900	William Jennings Bryan	137	861,459
28.	1904	Alton B. Parker	196	2,544,343
29.	1908	William Jennings Bryan	159	1,269,900
30.	1912	Theodore Roosevelt (Prog.)	347	2,070,194
31.	1916	Charles Evans Hughes	23	591,385
32.	1920	James Cox	277	7,004,847
33.	1924	John Davis	246	7,339,430
34.	1928	Alfred Smith	357	6,375,747

THE BOOK OF LOSERS

35.	1932	Herbert Hoover	413	7,060,016
36.	1936	Alfred Landon	515	11,072,014
37.	1940	Wendell Willkie	367	4,938,711
38.	1944	Thomas Dewey	333	3,596,227
39.	1948	Thomas Dewey	114	2,135,747
40.	1952	Adlai Stevenson	353	6,621,260
41.	1956	Adlai Stevenson	384	9,553,994
42.	1960	Richard Nixon	84	118,550
43.	1964	Barry Goldwater	434	15,949,707
44.	1968	Hubert Humphrey	110	510,314
45.	1972	George McGovern	503	17,997,124
46.	1976	Gerald Ford	56	1,743,410

Source: *The World Almanac*, 1979, New York: Newspaper Enterprise Assn. 1979.

PRESIDENTIAL LOSERS

In the game of life, it's a good idea to have a few early losses, which relieves you of the pressure of trying to maintain an undefeated season.

BILL VAUGHN

1. George Washington (1732–1799)

In 1755 and 1757, Washington lost races for the Virginia House of Burgesses.

POLITICAL LOSERS 81

2. John Adams (1735–1826)
Adams lost the 1800 presidential election to Thomas Jefferson.

3. Thomas Jefferson (1743–1826)
Jefferson lost the presidential election in 1796 to John Adams.

4. James Madison (1751–1836)
Madison lost a 1777 race for the Virginia Assembly.

5. James Monroe (1758–1831)
Monroe lost the presidential election in 1808 to James Madison.

6. John Quincy Adams (1767–1848)
Adams lost his 1828 presidential bid.

7. Andrew Jackson (1767–1845)
Jackson lost the 1824 presidential election even though he had the most popular votes and electoral votes. Since he didn't have a majority, the House of Representatives voted the presidency to John Quincy Adams.

8. Martin Van Buren (1782–1862)
Van Buren lost the 1840 presidential election to William Henry Harrison. In 1844, he lost the Democratic nomination to James Knox Polk. Four years later, as the nominee of the Free Soil Party, he lost another presidential election.

9. William Henry Harrison (1773–1841)
Among his many defeats, Harrison lost a race for governor of Ohio, and ran unsuccessfully for both houses of Congress.

10. John Tyler (1790–1862)
Tyler lost a race for vice-president in 1836.

THE BOOK OF LOSERS

11. James Polk (1795–1849)

Polk lost his bid for the vice-presidential nomination in 1840, and two races for governor.

12. Millard Fillmore (1800–1874)

Fillmore lost a race for governor of New York. He also lost an attempt to get the presidential nomination of the Whig Party in 1852. In 1856 he lost a presidential election as the candidate of the Know Nothing Party.

13. Franklin Pierce (1804–1869)

Pierce lost the Democratic nomination for President in 1856.

14. James Buchanan (1791–1868)

Buchanan lost on three attempts to win the Democratic presidential nomination—in 1844, 1848, 1852.

15. Abraham Lincoln (1809–1865)

Lincoln lost a race for the state legislature of Illinois. He also lost a race for the U.S. Senate. In 1856, he lost a race for the Republican vice-presidential nomination.

16. Andrew Johnson (1808–1875)

Johnson lost a race for the state legislature, as well as a race for Congress.

17. Ulysses S. Grant (1822–1885)

Grant lost a hard-fought attempt to win his third Republican nomination for the presidency in 1880.

18. Rutherford B. Hayes (1822–1893)

Hayes lost a race for Congress in 1872.

POLITICAL LOSERS 83

19. Chester A. Arthur (1829–1886)
Arthur was defeated for the Republican presidential renomination in 1884.

20. Grover Cleveland (1837–1908)
Cleveland lost the 1888 presidential election, despite having more popular votes than Benjamin Harrison.

21. Benjamin Harrison (1833–1901)
Harrison lost the 1876 race for governor of Indiana, and a later race for the U.S. Senate. He also lost the presidential race in 1892 to Cleveland.

22. William McKinley (1843–1901)
McKinley lost two races for the U.S. House of Representatives from Ohio.

23. Theodore Roosevelt (1858–1919)
Roosevelt lost a race for mayor of New York. He also lost the presidential race in 1912 as the candidate of the Bull Moose Party.

24. William Howard Taft (1857–1930)
Taft lost the 1912 presidential election to Woodrow Wilson.

25. Warren Harding (1865–1923)
Harding lost an early race for county auditor, but went on to lose a race for governor of Ohio.

26. Calvin Coolidge (1872–1933)
In 1905 Coolidge lost an election for school committeeman of Northhampton, Vermont.

84   *THE BOOK OF LOSERS*

27. Herbert Hoover (1874–1964)
Hoover lost the 1932 presidential reelection to Franklin Roosevelt.

28. Franklin Roosevelt (1882–1945)
Running for vice-president in 1920, Roosevelt and his running mate Cox were defeated.

29. Harry Truman (1884–1972)
Truman lost a race for judgeship of Jackson County Court, Missouri.

30. John F. Kennedy (1917–1963)
Kennedy lost an attempt for the 1956 vice-presidential nomination.

31. Lyndon Johnson (1908–1973)
Johnson lost a U.S. Senate race in Texas, and went on to lose his bid for the 1960 Democratic presidential nomination.

32. Richard Nixon (1913–)
Nixon was defeated in the 1960 presidential election, and again two years later in the California gubernatorial election.

33. Gerald Ford (1913–)
Ford lost the 1976 race for President.

34. Jimmy Carter (1924–)
Carter lost a 1966 race for governor of Georgia.

Note: Zachary Taylor, James Garfield, Woodrow Wilson, and Dwight Eisenhower were the only Presidents who never lost an attempt at office.

Source: The information for this section is taken from numerous historical accounts.

–IV–
Military Losers

THE LOSERS OF CREASY'S FIFTEEN MOST DECISIVE BATTLES

In war, whichever side may call itself the victor, there are no winners, but all are losers.
NEVILLE CHAMBERLAIN, "Speech at Kettering"

1. The Battle of Marathon (Greek–Persian Wars, 490 B.C.)

King Darius I led his 100,000 Persians to a mighty defeat at the hands of 10,000 Athenians under Miltiades. During the course of the battle, the invincible Persians killed 192 of their spirited enemy while losing only 6,000 of their men.

2. The Battle of Syracuse (Peloponnesian Wars, 413 B.C.)

Athenian dominance ended forever with their devastating defeat at Syracuse. Led by Alcibiades, the Athenians amassed a huge armada of 134 warships and began a one-year siege against Syracuse. Nonetheless, the citizens of the city held on, and a relief column from Sparta under Gylippus broke through the siege lines and routed the Athenian force.

85

86   THE BOOK OF LOSERS

3. The Battle of Metaurus (Punic Wars, 207 B.C.)

The city of Carthage lost its best chance to capture Rome when its large army under Hasdrubal and Hannibal was crushed by the Romans under Gaius Claudius. Despite having a far superior number of men at the point of attack, the Carthaginians were surprised while fording the river Metaurus and managed to have more men killed (10,000) than the attacking contingent of Romans had men (7,000).

4. The Battle of Arbela (Macedonian Wars of Expansion, 331 B.C.)

Not to be outdone by Darius I, King Darius III showed his complete military incompetence in battle with Alexander the Great. In 333 B.C., he lost to Alexander at Issus by disorganizing his army through a premature personal retreat (he also lost his wife, reported to be the most beautiful in Asia, to the Macedonian). Not content with one defeat, he opened the gates of Asia to Alexander when he allowed Alexander's 47,000-man army to decisively defeat his Persian force of 150,000 at Arbela.

5. The Battle of Teutoburg Forest (Roman–Germanic Wars, A.D. 9)

Rome had its hunger for additional German lands ended permanently after a disastrous piece of generalship by Varus. The shrewd Varus allowed his 50,000 Romans to be lured into the Teutoberg forest and surrounded by the German Arminius. There they were systematically slaughtered (with the exception of Varus, who committed suicide, and a small group of soldiers who were enslaved).

6. The Battle of Chalon-sur-Marne (Roman–Hunnish Wars, 451)

In one of his few defeats, Attila led 40,000 Huns to defeat at this crucial battle, which determined the course of Western

MILITARY LOSERS

87

Europe. Flavius Aetius, Roman commander, and Theodoric I, German Visigoth, drove the Huns back across the Rhine.

7. The Battle of Tours (Moslem invasion of Southwest Europe, 732)

After successfully annexing countries from India to the Atlantic Ocean, the Moslems finally lost at Tours and were thrown back into Spain. Though superior in numbers, the 90,000 cavalry men led by Abdar-Rahman were defeated by the Merovingian mayor Charles Martel and his heavy-armed cavalry. After Tours, the armored knight with lance became a common sight on European battlefields.

8. The Battle of Hastings (Norman invasion of England, 1066)

King Harold defeated his brother in September 1066 at Stamford Bridge, England. The defeat was convincing, but weakened his troops. They were further weakened by a 200-mile forced march which Harold orderd so he could meet William at Hastings. Even so, Harold chose a strong defensive position, and his 9,000-man Saxon infantry repelled numerous charges by William's 7,000-man cavalry. Finally, however, William duped Harold into believing he had ordered a retreat. The Saxons broke ranks; the Normans returned and conquered them. Harold died, pierced through the eye by an arrow.

9. The Battle of Orleans (Hundred Years' War, 1429)

The English forces, generaled by the Duke of Bedford and Earl of Salisbury, allowed their superstitions to stop them. Believing in the prophecy that France would be redeemed by a virgin, the English were convinced that Joan was a witch and they fought poorly against her inspired forces, totaling about 7,000. Though she was no military leader or tactician, her reckless courage helped rout the English at Orleans, the turning point in the war.

THE BOOK OF LOSERS

10. The Battle of Blenheim (War of Spanish Succession, 1704)

The 60,000-man Franco-Bavarian force under Louis XIV was no match for the 50,000-man army of the Duke of Marlborough and Prince Eugene of Savoy. Superior generalship decided the day with 24,000 French dead against "only" 11,000 for the allied troops, and ended French hopes for European rule.

11. The Battle of Poltava (Russo–Swedish War, 1709)

Swedish King Charles XII had plans too grandiose for his small state. After successfully invading the Ukraine, he decided to fight the Russians at Poltava, though outnumbered 50,000 to 20,000. His Swedes were slaughtered, only 1,500 surviving.

12. The Battle of the Spanish Armada (English–Spanish Wars, 1588)

In a masterpiece of ineptitude, Philip II's 132–ship, 33,000-soldier navy was utterly destroyed by the 34-ship English fleet under Sir Francis Drake. By the end of the battle, only fifty Spanish ships were afloat, and English naval power was supreme.

13. The Battle of Saratoga (American Revolution, 1777)

The British overcame the poor leadership of American general Horatio Gates en route to their crucial defeat at the hands of American forces. This victory was made easier by the failure of General Henry Clinton and his 15,000 soldiers to support General Burgoyne's 6,000 troops. Burgoyne's British soldiers were surrounded at Saratoga when the Americans cut off their escape route. The ensuing surrender of 5,790 British veterans gave new inspiration to sagging American morale.

14. The Battle of Valmy (French Revolution, 1792)

The Revolutionary Government of France was secured by the Prussian loss at Valmy. The opposing forces were about equal:

MILITARY LOSERS 89

36,000 French led by Domouriez against the 34,000 Prussians. There was little hand-to-hand contact, but the Duke of Brunswick's troops retreated after an intense artillery duel.

15. The Battle of Waterloo (Napoleonic Wars, 1815)

Though numerically superior, Napoleon's force of 71,947 men and 246 guns lost to an allied force of 67,655 men with 156 guns under the Duke of Wellington. Both sides lost approximately 25,000 men, but the French were finally routed from the field. Disorganized and dispirited, they ceased to be an effective fighting force.

Source: Edward S. Creasy, *The 15 Decisive Battles of the World.* Simpkins, Marshal, Hamilton, Kent, 1890.

COUNTRIES THAT LOST THE MOST MEN IN WORD WAR I

They went forth to battle, but they always fell.
OSSIAN, *Cath-loda*

	Men Lost	Country
1.	1,773,700	Germany
2.	1,700,000	Russia
3.	1,357,800	France
4.	1,200,000	Austria–Hungary
5.	908,371	British Empire
6.	650,000	Italy
7.	335,706	Romania
8.	325,000	Turkey
9.	116,516	United States

Source of raw data: *Information Please Almanac: Atlas and Yearbook 1978.* New York, Information Please Pub. Inc., 1977.

Five Countries In Whose Army A Soldier Had The Greatest Chance Of Losing His Life In World War I

Odds against being killed	Country
5 to 4	Romania
5 to 1	Germany
5 to 1	France
11 to 2	Austria–Hungary
6 to 1	Russia

Source of raw data: David S. Neft, et al., *The World Book of Odds*. New York: Grosset & Dunlap, 1978.

Countries That Lost The Most Men In World War II (battle deaths only)

Men Lost	Country
6,115,000	Soviet Union
3,250,000	Germany
1,324,516	China
1,270,000	Japan
664,000	Poland
357,116	Britain
350,000	Romania
305,000	Yugoslavia

MILITARY LOSERS 91

291,557   United States
280,000   Austria

Source of raw data: *Information Please Almanac: Atlas and Yearbook 1978.* New York: Information Please Pub. Inc., 1977.

FIVE COUNTRIES IN WHOSE ARMY A SOLDIER HAD THE GREATEST CHANCE OF LOSING HIS LIFE IN WORLD WAR II (BATTLE DEATHS ONLY) *

Odds against being killed	*Country*
Even	Romania
2 to 1	Austria
5 to 1	Finland
7 to 1	Japan
11 to 1	Yugoslavia

* There are no accurate figures of how many men fought for the U.S.S.R.; German deaths were not broken down further than "deaths from all causes."

Source of raw data: David S. Neft, et al., *The World Book of Odds.* New York: Grosset & Dunlap, 1978.

FIVE WARS IN WHICH THE UNITED STATES LOST THE MOST MEN

Men Lost	War
529,332,(364,511 Union forces; 164,821 Confederate forces)	Civil War
405,399	World War II
116,516	World War I
56,962	Vietnam
54,246	Korean

Source of raw data: *Information Please Almanac: Atlas and Yearbook 1978.* New York: Information Please Pub. Inc., 1977.

ODDS AGAINST A MEMBER OF A PARTICULAR BRANCH OF THE U.S. MILITARY LOSING HIS LIFE IN A WAR

Odds	Branch, War
5 to 1	Army, Civil War
16 to 1	Marines + Navy, Civil War
26 to 1	Marines, World War II
27 to 1	Marines, World War I
34 to 1	Army, World War II

MILITARY LOSERS 93

37 to 1	Air Force + Army, World War I
53 to 1	Marines, Vietnam
66 to 1	Navy, World War II
75 to 1	Marines, Korea
75 to 1	Army, Korea

Source of raw data: David S. Neft, *The World Book of Odds*. New York: Grosset & Dunlap, 1978.

U.S. Urban Areas in Which You Have a "High Risk" of Being Killed By a Direct Hit from Nuclear Weapons and/ or Heavy Radioactive Fallout in World War III*

Alabama
Gasden
Birmingham
Huntsville
Mobile
Montgomery
Tuscaloosa

Alaska
Anchorage
Fairbanks

Arizona
Phoenix
Tucson

* Criteria for establishment as high risk included (in this order): military bases and installations, economic centers, dense population areas. Projections were based upon "Soviet capabilities (circa 1980) under existing Strategic Arms Limitation agreements and U.S. target values . . ."

94   *THE BOOK OF LOSERS*

Arkansas
  Pine Bluff
  Little Rock–North Little Rock
  Fort Smith

California
  San Francisco–Oakland
  Fresno
  Bakersfield
  Los Angeles–Long Beach
  Salinas
  Seaside–Monterey
  Sacramento
  San Bernardino–Riverside
  San Diego
  Stockton
  Santa Barbara
  San José
  Santa Rosa
  Modesto
  Oxnard–Ventura–Thousand
    Oaks
  Simi Valley

Colorado
  Boulder
  Denver
  Colorado Springs
  Pueblo

Connecticut
  Bridgeport
  Danbury
  Norwalk
  Stamford
  Bristol

  Hartford
  New Britain
  Mediden
  New Haven
  Waterbury

Delaware
  Wilmington

Florida
  Gainesville
  Fort Lauderdale–Hollywood
  Miami
  Jacksonville
  Pensacola
  Tampa
  Tallahassee
  Orlando
  West Palm Beach
  St. Petersburg

Georgia
  Macon
  Savannah
  Albany
  Atlanta
  Columbus
  Augusta

Hawaii
  Honolulu

Idaho
  Boise City

MILITARY LOSERS

Illinois
Champaign–Urbana
Chicago–Northwestern Indiana
Aurora–Elgin
Bloomington–Normal
Decatur
Peoria
Davenport–Rock
  Island–Moline
Springfield
Joliet
Rockford

Indiana
Fort Wayne
Muncie
Anderson
Indianapolis
South Bend
Lafayette–West Lafayette
Evansville
Terre Haute

Iowa
Waterloo
Dubuque
Cedar Rapids
Des Moines
Sioux City

Kansas
Wichita
Topeka

Kentucky
Owensboro

Lexington
Louisville

Louisiana
Shreveport
Lake Charles
Baton Rouge
Lafayette
New Orleans
Monroe

Maine
Lewiston–Auburn
Portland

Maryland
Baltimore

Massachusetts
Pittsfield
New Bedford
Lawrence–Haverhill
Springfield–Chicopee–Holyoke
Boston
Lowell
Brockton
Fitchburg–Leominster
Worcester

Michigan
Bay City
Flint
Lansing
Jackson
Kalamazoo
Grand Rapids

THE BOOK OF LOSERS

Muskegon–Muskegon Heights
Saginaw
Ann Arbor
Detroit

Minnesota
Minneapolis–St. Paul
Rochester
Duluth–Superior

Mississippi
Biloxi–Gulfport
Jackson

Missouri
Columbia
St. Joseph
Springfield
Kansas City
St. Louis

Montana
Great Falls
Billings

Nebraska
Omaha
Lincoln

Nevada
Las Vegas
Reno

New Hampshire
Manchester
Nashua

New Jersey
Atlantic City
Vineland–Millville
Trenton

New Mexico
Albuquerque

New York
Albany–Schenectady–Troy
Binghamton
Buffalo
New York–East New Jersey
Rochester
Utica–Rome
Syracuse

North Carolina
Asheville
Fayetteville
Durham
Winston–Salem
Greensboro
Highpoint
Charlotte
Wilmington
Raleigh

North Dakota
Fargo–Moorhead

Ohio
Lima
Hamilton
Springfield
Cleveland
Columbus

MILITARY LOSERS

Cincinnati
Steubenville–Weirton
Lorain–Elyria
Toledo
Youngstown–Warren
Dayton
Mansfield
Canton
Akron

Oklahoma
Lawton
Oklahoma City
Tulsa

Oregon
Eugene
Salem
Portland

Pennsylvania
Pittsburgh
Reading
Altoona
Johnstown
Harrisburg
Erie
Scranton
Lancaster
Allentown–Bethlehem–Easton
Wilkes-Barre
Philadelphia

Rhode Island
Providence–Pawtucket–War-
    wick

South Carolina
Charleston
Greenville
Columbia

South Dakota
Sioux Falls

Tennessee
Nashville–Davidson
Chattanooga
Knoxville
Memphis

Texas
San Antonio
Texarkana
Bryan–College Station
Brownsville
Harlington–San Benito
Dallas
Odessa
El Paso
Galveston
Texas City–La Marque
Sherman–Denison
Houston
McAllen–Pharr–Edinburg
Beaumont
Port Arthur
Lubbock
Waco
Midland
Corpus Christi
Amarillo
Tyler
Fort Worth

98 THE BOOK OF LOSERS

Abilene
San Angelo
Austin
Laredo
Wichita Falls

Utah
Salt Lake City
Provo–Orem
Ogden

Virginia
Lynchburg
Newport News–Hampton
Norfolk–Portsmouth
Petersburg–Colonial Heights
Richmond
Roanoke

Washington
Seattle–Everett

Tacoma
Spokane

West Virginia
Huntington–Ashland
Charleston
Wheeling

Wisconsin
Green Bay
Madison
Kenosha
Lacrosse
Milwaukee
Appleton
Racine
Oshkosh

District of Columbia
Washington

Source: U.S. Government Defense Civil Preparedness Agency, *High Risk Areas.* (TR-82, April, 1975).

–V–

Money Losers

Eleven Great Gambling Losers

Nothing stings more sharply than the loss of money.
Livy, *History XXX*

1. Yudihidhthira (Yudi) Pandavas, Indian rajah (1500 B.C.)

The Pandavas were challenged to a gambling match with the Kauravas—with the stakes being the possession of the Indian kingdom which the two families controlled. More than this, the Kauravas were jealous of the immense Pandavas fortune, and were determined to get it in any way possible. The Pandavas accepted the challenge, unaware that Sakuni Kaurava had a pair of loaded dice. Yudi Pandavas proceeded to lose every game, losing 100,000 slaves, and 100,000 slave girls covered with riches, and eventually his kingdom. However, he did not stop, and gambled away his brothers' fortunes, his brothers, and finally himself. Sakuni finally induced him to one last throw: all of his losses against Yudi's beautiful wife, Draupadi. Of course he lost that throw too.[1]

THE BOOK OF LOSERS

2. Nero, Roman emperor (37–68 A.D.)

Like his predecessor Claudius, who had his carriage altered so that he could throw dice while riding, Nero was obsessed with all types of dice games. No accurate records exist of his total losses, but Nero frequently lost sums as large as 400,000 *sestertii* (about $50,000) on a single throw.[1]

3. Henry VIII, king of England (1491–1547), and St. Paul's Church, London

The king enjoyed all forms of gambling, and would gamble for anything, whether his or not. The English historian Stow records that on one particularly unlucky day, Henry lost the bells of St. Paul's Church in a dice game with Sir Miles Partridge.[1]

4. Casanova de Seingalt, Italian author (1725–1798)

When not occupied with romantic endeavors, Casanova usually passed his time at European gaming houses. During one evening he managed to lose 5,000 gold sequins in a Venetian casino. Undaunted, the great seducer recouped his losses the next day with a stake from his lover of the moment.[1]

5. Louis M. Cohn and the city of Chicago (1871)

A crap game was going on in the O'Learys' barn when one gambler, Louis M. Cohn, was caught up in some excitement, and tipped over a lantern that was providing the light. After the great fire was over, Cohn dreamed up the story about the cow. It was only after his death, in 1944, that Cohn admitted his responsibility in his will, and left Northwestern University $35,000 as partial recompense.[1]

MONEY LOSERS

101

6. John Wayne "Bet-a-Million" Gates, American speculator (1855–1911)

Gates was an inveterate gambler; he once won $22,000 on a rainy-day train ride by betting on which raindrop would slide down the window first. One day in the summer of 1902, he lost $375,000 at New York's Saratoga Race Track. Undaunted, he had dinner, then went to the Club House to play faro. He proceeded to lose another $150,000. This would have stopped a lesser man, but Gates fought back and won $300,000, making his net loss for the day only $225,000.[1]

7. Janzieska and Roszieska Deutsch, Hungarian cabaret artists

These two sisters made friends with Gordon Selfridge, the English millionaire; for twenty-five years they lived with him and lost the equivalent of $8,000,000. Selfridge finally became bankrupt.[1]

8. Nicholas Zographos, Greek gambler

A member of the notorious Greek syndicate in Monte Carlo in the 1920s, Zographos had numerous disastrous gambling experiences, but always emerged successful. For example, an American gambler once challenged him to play one hand for 1,000,000 francs ($168,000). Zographos agreed, but only if the gambler agreed to the best out of three. Zographos went on to lose the first, but calmly returned and won the next two. However, during one 1926 week in Cannes, he lost $672,000. This left him with only a million francs, from which he was able to build another fortune.[1]

9. Andre Citroën, French automobile manufacturer (1878–1935)

Fond of attention, Citroën went on a baccarat binge one night in 1926. Determined to set a record for one of the biggest losses

102   THE BOOK OF LOSERS

in one session in history, he succeeded by losing 13 million francs ($500,000) that night.[1]

10. Farouk, King of Egypt (1920–1965)

Farouk's obsessive gambling led him to the casinos of Monaco, where he lost money with the world's richest men after his abdication. Obviously wealthy, Farouk had special tables reserved for his personal use. The casinos took the extraordinary step of imposing no maximum stakes on the ex-king who used £1,000 chips to bet. At the height of his sprees, he would employ his staff as runners so that he could gamble on numerous tables simultaneously. During one memorable evening, Farouk's bad luck exceeded even his normal misfortune, as he lost £55,000 at the Deauville Casino.[2]

11. Nicholas Andrea Dandolos (Nick the Greek) (1882–1966)

Stories about the legendary Greek abound. He was an enormous draw at all casinos he visited because of his penchant to keep on playing after he had lost over $100,000 at a single sitting (which he did frequently). It has been estimated that $500,000,000 "passed through his hands"; he said that he had been wealthy and flat broke at least seventy-three times. On one memorable evening, the Greek lost the biggest pot in the history of stud poker, $797,000, to Arnold Rothstein—the gambler who fixed the 1919 World Series.[3]

SOURCES:
1. Alan Wykes, *The Complete Illustrated Guide to Gambling*. Garden City: Doubleday & Co., 1964.
2. Hugh McLeave, *The Last Pharaoh: Farouk of Egypt*. New York: McCall, 1969.
3. Cy Rice, *Nick the Greek: King of the Gamblers*. New York: Funk & Wagnalls, 1969.

MONEY LOSERS

LOST SUNKEN TREASURE IN THE WESTERN HEMISPHERE

During the time when the European colonial powers were stripping the New World of its riches, numerous galleons met untimely ends—either at the hands of pirates and raiders from other countries, or from storms. The following list does not purport to be comprehensive but it is a representative sampling of some of the major lost treasures waiting to be found.

1. Spanish galleon, *San José:* over 11,000,000 pesos lost (1708)

This ship was the richest Spanish vessel ever lost in the Western Hemisphere. En route from South America to Spain, the fleet, of which the *San José* was the main ship, was intercepted by the English. A long battle ensued, with the English emerging victorious. The *San José* exploded and sank near Bara Island, but the exact location was not documented. Its treasure remains lost there today.

2. Spanish galleons, *Capitana, San Roque, Almiranta, Santo Domingo; Nuestra Señora de Begonia, San Ambrosia:* around 8,000,000 pesos lost (1605)

These ships were part of a fleet that was partially sunk by a hurricane off the coast of Central America (between the Serrana and Sevanilla banks) while on their way from Cartagena to Spain. The Spanish attempted to discover the location of the wrecks immediately thereafter, but were unsuccessful. Over sixty years later Cuban fishermen happened upon the wrecks by chance, and salvaged some coins from two of the lost ships. Terrible weather has made subsequent salvage operations impossible.

104   THE BOOK OF LOSERS

3. Spanish galleon, *Invincible:* 4,000,000 pesos lost (1740)

This ship did not succumb to pirates or foul weather, but rather to a bolt of lightning which struck while it was moored in Havana harbor. The resulting explosion obliterated the ship and much of the city around the harbor. Its huge treasure is lost on the bed of the harbor.

4. Spanish galleons, *Capitana, Nuestra Señora del Juncal, Almiranta,* and the smaller *naos* of Captains Espinosa, Amesqueta, and Niculas: around 3,500,000 pesos lost (1631)

Making its way from Veracruz to Havana, this Spanish fleet was hit by a vicious hurricane off the coast of Mexico—around eight leagues north of the Bajo de Castucas. Some coins were salvaged from one of the *naos,* but the bulk of the treasure remains lost. The exact location of the wrecks of the largest ships was never discovered.

5. Spanish galleon, *Nuestra Señora da la Maravillas:* about 3,500,000 pesos lost (1656)

In another bizarre incident, the entire fleet of which this ship was a member ranged into shallow water one night and had to turn precipitously seaward. As a result, the *Nuestro Señora* rammed another galleon and sank on the Little Bahama Bank, about twenty miles north of Memory Rock. Recovery operations netted about 1.5 million pesos of the 5-million-peso cargo; the remainder of the treasure was lost to shifting sands.

6. New Spain Flota, consisting of six ships: nearly 3,000,000 pesos lost (1657)

In an attempt to elude English raiders on a return trip from Veracruz to Spain, the fleet encountered fierce weather near Puerto Rico. As a result, six of the ships were lost near Dominica. Some survivors escaped with a small portion of the

MONEY LOSERS 105

treasure, but they were butchered by natives as they swam ashore. None of the treasure has been seen since.

7. Spanish galleon, *Capitana:* about 3,000,000 pesos lost (1654)

Carrying booty from South American mines, the ship left Callao for Panama. One stormy evening the galleon wrecked on Chandvy Reef, near the mouth of Ecuador's Guayaquil River. A small amount of treasure was located before sand covered the rest.

8. Spanish galleon, *Espiritu Santa el Mayor:* more than 1,000,000 pesos lost (1623)

This galleon was part of a fleet that met the same fate as many others; it was sunk by a tremendous storm near the mouth of the Bahama Channel. Other ships in the fleet were luckier, and their treasures were salvaged; however, the *Espiritu Santa el Mayor* went down so quickly that none of its treasure was recovered.

9. Two Spanish fleets: around 1,000,000 pesos lost (1715)

These treasure-laden fleets were on their way from Havana to Spain via the infamous Bahama Channel. A huge hurricane sank all of the ships but one, on the coast of Florida. Over 5 million pesos were salvaged from the wrecks, but the Spaniards reportedly left approximately 1 million pesos.

10. Spanish návio, *San Nicholás:* about 1,000,000 pesos lost (1647)

A tremendous earthquake hit Peru and Chile, causing numerous ships to capsize in the two countries' ports. At Arica, Chile, the *San Nicholás* went down, and to date divers have been able to recover only a small part of the treasure.

Source: Robert Marx, *Shipwrecks of the Western Hemisphere (1492-1825).* New York: World Publishing Co., 1971.

Ten Outrageous Losses of Taxpayer Money (Selected Winners of Senator William Proxmire's "Golden Fleece Awards")

Since March 1975, Senator William Proxmire of Wisconsin has made monthly "Golden Fleece Awards," awarded "to the biggest, most ridiculous, or most ironic examples of government spending or waste."

1. March 1975 Recipient: National Science Foundation; Amount lost—$84,000

Proxmire made this award on the basis of the foundation's study of why people fall in love. Wrote Proxmire: "I object to this because no one—not even the National Science Foundation—can argue that falling in love is a science. Even if they spent $84 million or $84 billion, they wouldn't get an answer that anyone would believe. . . . I believe that 200 million other Americans want to leave some things in life a mystery, and right at the top of the list of things we don't want to know is why a man falls in love with a woman and vice versa."

2. August 1975 Recipient: Federal Aviation Administration; Amount lost—$57,800

In this landmark study, the FAA compiled a 103-page report on the body measurements of 423 American Airlines stewardess trainees. A series of seventy-nine measurements was made on each woman by some undoubtedly jubilant measurer. Various

MONEY LOSERS

measurements included "the knee to knee breadth while sitting" and "the popliteal length of the buttocks." The ostensible reason for the research was to help establish the design for safety equipment, but as Proxmire pointed out, the sample was "unrepresentative . . . and completely useless."

3. October 1975 Recipient: National Institute on Alcohol Abuse and Alcoholism; Amount lost—$192,000

The questions posed by two NIAA studies were: (1) Are drunk fish more aggressive than sober fish? and (2) Can rats be turned into alcoholics, and if so will young rats drink more than adult rats to relieve anxiety? To answer the first question, a particularly lucky species of sunfish sipped gin and tequila. In the second case, the poor rats were shocked unpredictably in an attempt to make them neurotic. Proxmire stated: " . . . The fish and rats are so much lower on the evolutionary scale than man that the result of these experiements will tell us very little, if anything, about the nature of complex human problems such as alcoholism."

4. January 1977 Recipient: Department of Agriculture; Amount lost—$46,000

The department hired a group of researchers to find out how long it takes to cook breakfast. To sophisticate their results, the researchers created a "time measurement unit" which was equal to .036 seconds. As to the results which all taxpayers will be able to use: it takes 838 TMUs to fry two eggs, 1,222 TMUs to produce six ounces of hash, and 960 TMUs to fix a piece of French toast. More than this, in the egg-frying process is included 22 TMUs to get the egg, 15 TMUs to break it on the bowl and so forth.

108   *THE BOOK OF LOSERS*

5. February 1977 Recipient: Law Enforcement Assistance Administration; Amount lost—$27,000

The administration financed a study to answer the monumentally difficult question: Why do inmates want to escape from prison? Aside from the obvious absurdity involved, Proxmire also demonstrated how the obscure language of the results completely erased any usefulness the study might have had: "The increase in predictability of escape from $R = .64$ when secondary variables are used singly and $R = .61$ when questionnaire variables are used singly to $R = .77$ when both are used co-jointly, empirically demonstrates that escape is associated with both static and dynamic factors."

6. May 1977 Recipient: National Endowment for the Humanities; Amount lost—$2,500

This NEH grant was awarded to the city of Arlington, Virginia, to find out why "people are rude, cheat, and lie on the local tennis courts." The money was spent to hire a professor of sociology and a professor of ethics and philosophy, and to conduct two public meetings in which the professors guided some local tennis enthusiasts in role-playing activities.

7. September 1977 Recipient: National Endowment for the Arts; Amount lost—$6,025

This money was paid to an artist to film "the throwing of crepe paper" out of an airplane. Four one-mile-long crepe-paper rolls were thrown out of two planes over El Paso; the paper was then unfurled by sky divers who accompanied them on their trip to the ground. The grant also included money to pay a ground crew to clean up the mess.

MONEY LOSERS

109

8. March 1978 Recipient: United States Senate; Amount lost—$122,000,000

The Senate received the award because of the incredible cost overruns on the "frivolous" new office buildings it was building for itself. Originally, the building, which included a rooftop restaurant and three gymnasiums, was to cost $47 million, but according to Proxmire "built-in incentives to spend, delays coupled with rising costs, and the addition of unnecessary luxuries" almost tripled the original estimate.

9. April 1978 Recipient: National Institute for Mental health (NIMH); Amount lost—$97,000

Part of this grant went to a study of a Peruvian brothel, in which prostitutes were interviewed and observed, and the madam was extensively researched. The premise for the overall study was "to study ethnic and class relationships among Indians and non-Indians in several communities in the Peruvian Andes."

10. June 1978 Recipient: Federal Highway Administration (FHA); Amount lost—$222,000

The administration funded a study entitled "Motorist Attitudes Toward Large Trucks." A sampling of the burning questions asked includes: (1) Do you consider that large trucks contribute to traffic congestion? (2) Do you consider that large trucks block a driver's vision? Moreover, this study was completed as a companion to the $1 million study of "The Effect of Truck Size and Weight on Accident Experience and Traffic Operations" and a $297,633 study of "The Effects of Truck Size on Driver Behavior."

Source: Publications of Senator William Proxmire.

110 THE BOOK OF LOSERS

Twelve Cities (over 50,000 People) in Which Citizens Lose the Most Money to City Income Taxes

City	Maximum Rate
Washington, D.C.	11%
Philadelphia	4.3125%
New York	4.3%
Covington, Ky.	2.5%
Scranton, Pa.	2.5%
Detroit	2%
Gasden, Ala.	2%
Lexington, Ky.	2%
Louisville, Ky.	2%
Cincinnati	2%
Springfield, Ohio	2%
Wilkes-Barre, Pa.	2%

Source of raw data: Tax Foundation (1979).

TEN CITIES IN WHICH A FAMILY OF FOUR MAKING $20,000 LOSES THE GREATEST PERCENTAGE OF ITS INCOME TO STATE AND LOCAL TAXES (SALES, INCOME, AUTO, REAL ESTATE)

City	Percent Lost
New York	18.5%
Boston	15.8%
Milwaukee	14.7%
Buffalo	13.7%
Los Angeles	12.4%
San Francisco	11.6%
Detroit	10.3%
Chicago	10.0%
Pittsburgh	9.9%
Baltimore	9.7%

Source of raw data: *Statistical Abstract of the United States 1977.* Estimate (list based on selected large cities).

TEN STATES IN WHICH CITIZENS WITH AN INCOME OVER $20,000 LOSE THE MOST MONEY TO STATE INCOME TAXES (EXCLUDING EXEMPTIONS, AND STATES IN WHICH STATE INCOME TAX IS BASED ON FEDERAL INCOME TAX)

State	Rate
Minnesota	15%
New York	12%
California	11%
Hawaii	10.5%
District of Columbia	10%
Montana	10%
Oregon	10%
Wisconsin	9.5%
Maine	9.2%
Delaware	8.8%

Source of raw data: *The World Almanac, 1980.* New York: Newspaper Enterprise Assn., 1980.

TEN STATES IN WHICH CITIZENS LOSE THE MOST MONEY TO STATE GENERAL SALES AND USE TAXES

State	Rate
Connecticut	7%
Pennsylvania	6%
Rhode Island	6%
District of Columbia	5%
Kentucky	5%
Maine	5%
Maryland	5%
Massachusetts	5%
Mississippi	5%
New Jersey	5%

Source of raw data: *Information Please Almanac: Atlas and Yearbook, 1980.* New York: Information Please Pub. Inc., 1977.

114 THE BOOK OF LOSERS

BIGGEST LOSERS IN SALES AMONG THE TOP 500 U.S. CORPORATIONS (1973–1978)

No man profiteth but by the loss of others.
MONTAIGNE, *Essays*

Corporations	*Decrease in Sales %*
1973	
1. Boise Cascade (wood products)	22.6
2. Magnavox	9.6
3. Loews	8.7
4. Squibb (pharmaceuticals)	4.9
5. Maremont (motor vehicles)	2.9
1974	
1. Genesco (apparel)	16.0
2. Skyline (transportation equipment)	15.9
3. Fleetwood Enterprises (transportation equipment)	15.5
4. AMAX	13.0
5. General Motors	11.9
1975	
1. Kennecott Copper	53.8
2. National Vulcanized Fiber (metal manufacturing)	37.9
3. General Cable	37.0
4. Anaconda (metal manufacturing)	35.0
5. Tecumseh Products (industrial and farm equipment)	31.1

MONEY LOSERS 115

1976
1. AMSTAR (food)   33.7
2. Singer   17.2
3. Anderson, Clayton (food)   13.6
4. Studebaker Worthington   12.9
5. Anheuser-Busch   12.4

1977
1. Cook Industries (food)   19.8
2. AMSTAR (food)   15.0
3. United Merchants (textiles,
      vinyl flooring)   13.8
4. Westmoreland Coal   13.4
5. Commonwealth Oil   13.1

1978
1. United Merchants   34.5
2. Spencer Foods   32.3
3. Natomas   22.5
4. White Motor   19.2
5. Chicago Bridge and Iron   16.4
6. Hunt Intl. Resources   16.4

Source: *Fortune* magazine, May 1974–9.

116   *THE BOOK OF LOSERS*

LARGEST CORPORATE MONEY LOSERS IN THE U.S. (1973–1978)

Corporation	*Amount Lost*
1973	
1. Genesco	52,903,000
2. Mattel	32,387,000
3. Pitney-Bowes (office equipment)	22,416,000
4. Marathon Manufacturing (industrial and farm equipment)	18,912,000
5. AVCO (aerospace)	18,348,000
1974	
1. Chrysler	52.094,000
2. Evans Products (wood products)	44.414,000
3. United Brands (food)	43,607,000
4. Litton Industries (office equipment)	39,806,000
5. Bangor-Punta (transportation equipment)	34.506,000
1975	
1. Singer	451,900,000
2. Chrysler	259,535,000
3. White Motors	69,374,000
4. Anaconda	39,786,000
5. Scovill Manufacturing (electronics)	33,196,000

MONEY LOSERS 117

1976
1. Rohr Industries (aerospace)   52,124,000
2. American Motors   46,340,000
3. Commonwealth Oil   32,085,000
4. Warnaco (apparel)   23,326,000
5. United Merchants   19,854,000

1977
1. Bethlehem Steel   488,200,000
2. United Merchants   181,852,000
3. Lykes (metal manufacturing) 189,746,000
4. Genesco   135,783,000
5. Cook   81,051,000

1978
1. Chrysler   204,600,000
2. Firestone   148,300,000
3. Litton   90,843,000
4. Peabody Holding   54,545,000
5. Commonwealth Oil   53,854,000

Source: *Fortune* magazine, May 1974-9.

ELEVEN BIGGEST CORPORATE MONEY LOSERS IN THE U.S. (1973–1978)

The figure given is the sum of amounts lost during particular years between 1973 and 1978. It does not necessarily represent

118 THE BOOK OF LOSERS

net loss for the entire period, since a company may have made money one year which offset a loss the previous year.

1.	Chrysler	$516,229,000
2.	Bethlehem Steel	488,200,000
3.	Singer	462,000,000
4.	United Merchants (rev)	230,173,000
5.	Genesco	202,983,000
6.	Lykes	189,746,000
7.	Commonwealth Oil Ref.	128,149,000
8.	Cook Industries	81,051,000
9.	American Motors	73,840,000
10.	Tesoro Petroleum	58,133,000
11.	Mattel	57,706,000

Source: *Fortune* magazine, May 1974-9.

−VI−
Movie Star Losers

Hollywood is a place where people from Iowa mistake each other for stars.

FRED ALLEN

ACADEMY AWARD LOSERS THROUGH 1979

Losers of the "Best Actor" Award

1. *Three-time Losers*

   Montgomery Clift

   Gary Cooper

   Kirk Douglas

Nominated for:

The Search (1948)
A Place in the Sun (1951)
From Here to Eternity (1953)

Mr. Deeds Goes to Town (1936)
Pride of the Yankees (1942)
For Whom the Bell Tolls (1943)

Champion (1949)
The Bad and the Beautiful (1952)
Lust for Life (1956)

119

120 THE BOOK OF LOSERS

Dustin Hoffman	*The Graduate* (1967) *Midnight Cowboy* (1969) *Lenny* (1974)
Fredric March	*The Royal Family of Broadway* (1931) *A Star Is Born* (1937) *Death of a Salesman* (1951)
Jack Nicholson	*Five Easy Pieces* (1970) *The Last Detail* (1973) *Chinatown* (1974)
William Powell	*The Thin Man* (1934) *My Man Godfrey* (1936) *Life With Father* (1947)
2. *Four-time Losers*	*Nominated for:*
Charles Boyer	*Conquest* (1937) *Algiers* (1938) *Gaslight* (1944) *Fanny* (1961)
Paul Muni	*The Valiant* (1929) *I Am a Fugitive from a Chain Gang* (1933) *The Life of Emile Zola* (1937) *The Last Angry Man* (1959)
Paul Newman	*Cat on a Hot Tin Roof* (1958) *The Hustler* (1961) *Hud* (1963) *Cool Hand Luke* (1967)
Al Pacino	*Serpico* (1973) *The Godfather, Part II* (1974) *Dog Day Afternoon* (1975) *And Justice For All* (1979)

MOVIE STAR LOSERS   121

James Stewart	*Mr. Smith Goes to Washington* (1939) *It's a Wonderful Life* (1946) *Harvey* (1950) *Anatomy of a Murder* (1959)

3. *Five-time Losers*   *Nominated for:*

Marlon Brando

A Streetcar Named Desire (1951)
Viva Zapata! (1952)
Julius Caesar (1953)
Sayonara (1957)
Last Tango in Paris (1973)

Peter O'Toole

Lawrence of Arabia (1962)
Becket (1964)
The Lion in Winter (1968)
Goodbye, Mr. Chips (1969)
The Ruling Class (1972)

4. *Six-time Losers*   *Nominated for:*

Richard Burton

The Robe (1953)
Becket (1964)
The Spy Who Came in from the Cold (1965)
Who's Afraid of Virginia Woolf? (1966)
Anne of the Thousand Days (1969)
Equus (1977)

Spencer Tracy

San Francisco (1936)
Father of the Bride (1950)
Bad Day at Black Rock (1955)
The Old Man and the Sea (1958)
Judgment at Nuremberg (1961)
Guess Who's Coming to Dinner (1967)

122   *THE BOOK OF LOSERS*

5. *Seven-time Loser*

   Laurence Olivier

Nominated for:

Wuthering Heights (1939)
Rebecca (1940)
Henry V (1946)
Richard III (1956)
Othello (1965)
Sleuth (1972)
The Boys From Brazil (1978)

Losers of the "Best Actress" Award

1. *Three-time Losers*

   Anne Bancroft

Nominated for:

The Pumpkin Eater (1964)
The Graduate (1967)
The Turning Point (1977)

Greta Garbo

Anna Christie/Romance (1930)
Camille (1937)
Ninotchka (1939)

Jennifer Jones

Love Letters (1945)
Duel in the Sun (1946)
Love Is a Many-Splendored Thing
(1955)

Eleanor Parker

Caged (1950)
Detective Story (1951)
Interrupted Melody (1955)

Vanessa Redgrave

Morgan! (1966)
Isadora (1968)
Mary, Queen of Scots (1971)

Gloria Swanson

Sadie Thompson (1928)
The Trespasser (1930)
Sunset Boulevard (1950)

MOVIE STAR LOSERS 123

Elizabeth Taylor	*Raintree County* (1957) *Cat on a Hot Tin Roof* (1958) *Suddenly, Last Summer* (1959)
Jane Wyman	*The Yearling* (1946) *The Blue Veil* (1951) *Magnificent Obsession* (1954)

2. *Four-time Losers*   *Nominated for:*

Ingrid Bergman	*For Whom the Bell Tolls* (1943) *The Bells of St. Mary's* (1945) *Joan of Arc* (1948) *Autumn Sonata* (1978)
Susan Hayward	*Smash Up—The Story of a Woman* (1947) *My Foolish Heart* (1949) *With a Song in My Heart* (1952) *I'll Cry Tomorrow* (1955)
Audrey Hepburn	*Sabrina* (1954) *The Nun's Story* (1959) *Breakfast at Tiffany's* (1961) *Wait Until Dark* (1967)
Shirley MacLaine	*Some Came Running* (1958) *The Apartment* (1960) *Irma La Douce* (1963) *The Turning Point* (1977)
Rosalind Russell	*My Sister Eileen* (1942) *Sister Kenny* (1946) *Mourning Becomes Electra* (1947) *Auntie Mame* (1958)
Norma Shearer	*A Free Soul* (1931) *The Barretts of Wimpole Street* (1934)

124 THE BOOK OF LOSERS

	Romeo and Juliet (1936)
	Marie Antoinette (1938)
Barbara Stanwyck	*Stella Dallas* (1937)
	Ball of Fire (1941)
	Double Indemnity (1944)
	Sorry, Wrong Number (1948)
3. *Five-time Losers*	*Nominated for:*
Irene Dunne	*Cimarron* (1931)
	Theodora Goes Wild (1936)
	The Awful Truth (1937)
	Love Affair (1939)
	I Remember Mama (1948)
4. *Six-time Losers*	*Nominated for:*
Greer Garson	*Goodbye, Mr. Chips* (1939)
	Blossoms in the Dust (1941)
	Madame Curie (1943)
	Mrs. Parkington (1944)
	The Valley of Decision (1945)
	Sunrise at Campobello (1960)
Deborah Kerr	*Edward My Son* (1949)
	From Here to Eternity (1953)
	The King and I (1956)
	Heaven Knows, Mr. Allison (1957)
	Separate Tables (1958)
	The Sundowners (1960)
5. *Eight-time Losers*	*Nominated for:*
Bette Davis	*Dark Victory* (1939)
	The Letter (1940)
	The Little Foxes (1941)
	Now, Voyager (1942)

MOVIE STAR LOSERS   125

Mr. Skeffington (1944)
All About Eve (1950)
The Star (1952)
What Ever Happened to Baby Jane? (1962)

Katharine Hepburn

Alice Adams (1935)
The Philadelphia Story (1940)
Woman of the Year (1942)
The African Queen (1951)
Summertime (1955)
The Rainmaker (1956)
Suddenly, Last Summer (1959)
Long Day's Journey Into Night (1962)

–VII–

Sports Losers

Soon fades the spell, soon comes the night;
Say will it not then be the same,
Whether we played the black or white,
Whether we lost or won the game?
THOMAS BABINGTON, LORD MACAULEY,
Sermon in a Churchyard.

When the One Great Scorer comes to write against your
name—
He marks—not that you won or lost—but how you played the
game.

GRANTLAND RICE, *Alumnus Football*

FOOTBALL—COLLEGE LOSERS

1. Biggest Loser in a Major College Game

On October 7, 1916, Cumberland University of Lebanon, Tennessee, lost to Georgia Tech by a margin of 222 points (222–0).

Source: ed., Norris McWhirter, *1978 edition: Guinness Book of World Records.* New York: Bantam, 1977.

126

2. Longest Losing Streaks

Team	Years	Consecutive Games Lost
St. Paul's Poly. (Virginia)	1947–53	41 *
McCallister (Minnesota)	1974–78	40
Northland (Wisconsin)	1940–49	31
Kansas State	1945–48	28
Virginia	1958–60	28
Knox College	1931–34	27
Trenton, N.J., Teacher's College	1938–47	27
Hardin Simmons	1959–62	27
Albany College (Oregon)	1931–35	28

* This stretch of forty-one games includes twenty-two straight games in which St. Paul's was outscored 890–0.

Primary Source: Frank G. Menke, *The Encyclopedia of Sports.* New York: A. S. Barnes, 1969.

3. Most Interceptions Suffered by a Quarterback

Most Passes Intercepted in One Game

In a 1969 game against Auburn, Florida quarterback John Reaves had nine passes intercepted.

Most Passes Intercepted in One Season

During the 1966 season, John Eckman of Wichita State threw a record thirty-four interceptions.

128   *THE BOOK OF LOSERS*

Most Passes Intercepted in a Career

Zeke Bratkowski of Georgia completed sixty-eight passes to opposing defensive secondaries throughout his fabled collegiate career.

Note: The NCAA does not keep records concerning fumbles by players and teams.

Source: National Collegiate Athletic Association.

4. Bowl Game Losers

Most Cotton Bowls Lost

The University of Texas, as the usual Southwest Conference representative, has steamrolled to seven Cotton Bowl losses (1951, 1960, 1963, 1971, 1972, 1974, 1978).

Biggest Loser in a Cotton Bowl Game

Texas Christian University (TCU): by a margin of 34 points in the 1945 game (34–0).

Most Sugar Bowls Lost

Louisiana State University has lost five of these New Orleans holiday classics (1936, 1937, 1938, 1950, 1960).

Biggest Loser in a Sugar Bowl Game

The LSU Tigers, by a margin of 35 points in the 1950 Sugar Bowl (35–0).

Most Orange Bowls Lost

Four teams have lost three games each: Alabama (1965, 1972, 1975); Miami (1934, 1935, 1951); Missouri (1940, 1960, 1970); Nebraska (1955, 1966, 1979).

SPORTS LOSERS 129

Biggest Loser in an Orange Bowl Game

Syracuse was demolished by a margin of 55 points in the 1953 game (61–6).

Most Rose Bowls Lost

The Trojans of Southern California have lost six games (1946, 1948, 1955, 1967, 1969, 1974).

Biggest Loser in a Rose Bowl Game

Tie: (a) Stanford lost the first Rose Bowl game by 49 points (49–0);

(b) U.S.C. plummeted to a 49-point defeat in the 1948 game (49-0).

Most Losses by a Team in Major Bowls

Ten losses by Alabama: Rose (1938); Cotton (1954, 1968, 1973); Sugar (1945, 1948, 1974); Orange (1965, 1972, 1975).

Most Consecutive Losses in Major Bowl Games

Four losses by Alabama: 1972 (Orange), 1973 (Cotton), 1974 (Sugar), 1975 (Orange).

Source of raw data: *The World Almanac, 1980.* New York: Newspaper Enterprise Assn., 1980.

130 THE BOOK OF LOSERS

FOOTBALL—PROFESSIONAL LOSERS

The twelve franchises with the highest losing percentages since their inception

Team (year) at least 12 seasons through 1979	Lost	Won	Tied	Losing %
New Orleans Saints (1967–79)	127	54	5	.682
Atlanta Falcons (1966–79)	124	72	4	.620
Brooklyn Dodgers/Tigers (1930–44)	100	60	9	.618
Denver Broncos (1960–79)	160	114	9	.565
Buffalo Bills (1960–79)	160	116	8	.563
Philadelphia Eagles (1933–79)	326	240	22	.554
New York Titans/Jets (1960–79)	156	122	6	.549
Chicago/St. Louis Cardinals (1920–79)	390	229	36	.537
Pittsburgh Pirates/Steelers (1933–79)	312	259	20	.527
San Francisco 49ers (1950–79)	210	180	12	.522
Houston Oilers (1960–79)	148	130	6	.521
Boston/New England Patriots (1960–79)	146	129	9	.514

Primary Source: *The NFL's Official Encyclopaedic History of Professional Football.* New York: MacMillan, 1976.

SPORTS LOSERS

131

All-Time Worst Teams 1921–1979 (at least ten games played)

Team, Year	Lost	Won	Tied	Winning %
1. Tampa Bay, 1976	14	0	0	.000
Detroit, 1942	11	0	0	.000
Dallas, 1960	11	0	1	.000
Chicago Cardinals, 1943	10	0	0	.000
Cardinals–Pittsburgh, 1944	10	0	0	.000
Brooklyn, 1944	10	0	0	.000
2. Oakland, 1962	13	1	0	.071
Pittsburgh, 1969	13	1	0	.071
Chicago, 1969	13	1	0	.071
Buffalo, 1971	13	1	0	.071
Houston, 1972	13	1	0	.071
Houston, 1973	13	1	0	.071
3. Washington, 1961	12	1	1	.077
Los Angeles, 1962	12	1	1	.077
New York Giants, 1966	12	1	1	.077
Atlanta, 1967	12	1	1	.077
Buffalo, 1968	12	1	1	.077
4. Philadelphia, 1936	11	1	0	.083
Baltimore, 1950	11	1	0	.083
Dallas, 1952	11	1	0	.083

Source of raw data: NFL Public Relations Department and Seymour Siwoff, ed., Fran Connors, *Official 1978 National Football League Record Manual*. National Football League, 1978.

Most Consecutive Games Lost

26: Tampa Bay, 1976–77
19: Chicago Cardinals, 1942–43, 1945
Oakland, 1961–62
18: Houston, 1972–73

Most Consecutive Games Without Victory

26: Tampa Bay, 1976–77 (lost 26)
23: Washington, 1960–61 (lost 20, tied 3)

Most Games Lost, Season (since 1932)

14: Tampa Bay, 1976
13: Oakland, 1962
Chicago, 1969
Pittsburgh, 1969
Buffalo, 1971
Houston, 1972; 1973
12: By many teams

Most Consecutive Games Lost, One Season

14: Tampa Bay, 1976
13: Oakland, 1962
12: Tampa Bay, 1977

Most Consecutive Games Lost, Start of Season

14: Tampa Bay, 1976, entire season
13: Oakland, 1962
12: Tampa Bay, 1977

SPORTS LOSERS 133

Most Consecutive Games Lost, End of Season

14: Tampa Bay, entire season
13: Pittsburgh, 1969
11: Philadelphia, 1936
Detroit, 1942, entire season
Houston, 1972

Most Consecutive Games Without Victory, One Season

14: Tampa Bay, 1976, entire season
13: Washington, 1961
Oakland, 1962
12: Dallas Cowboys, 1960, entire season
Tampa Bay, 1977

Most Passes Intercepted, Career

277: George Blanda, Chicago Bears, 1949–58; Baltimore, 1950; Houston, 1960–66; Oakland, 1967–75
268: John Hadl, San Diego, 1962–72; Los Angeles, 1973–74; Green Bay, 1974–75; Houston, 1976–77
257: Norm Snead, Washington, 1961–63; Philadelphia, 1964–70; Minnesota, 1971; New York Giants, 1972–74, 1976; San Francisco, 1974–75.

Most Passes Intercepted, Season

42: George Blanda, Houston, 1962
34: Frank Tripucka, Denver, 1960
32: John Hadl, San Diego, 1968

134   THE BOOK OF LOSERS

Most Passes Intercepted, Game

- 8: Jim Hardy, Chicago Cardinals vs. Philadelphia, Sept. 24, 1950
- 7: Parker Hall, Cleveland vs. Green Bay, Nov. 8, 1942
  Frank Sinkwich, Detroit vs. Green Bay, Oct. 24, 1943
  Bob Waterfield, Los Angeles vs. Green Bay, Oct. 17, 1948
  Zeke Bratkowski, Chicago vs. Baltimore, Oct. 2, 1960
  Tommy Wade, Pittsburgh vs. Philadelphia, Dec. 12, 1965
  Ken Stabler, Oakland vs. Denver, Oct. 16, 1977
- 6: By many players

Most Fumbles Lost, Career

- 105: Roman Gabriel, Los Angeles, 1962–72; Philadelphia, 1973–77
- 95: Johnny Unitas, Baltimore, 1956–72; San Diego, 1973
- 84: Len Dawson, Pittsburgh, 1957–59; Cleveland, 1960–61; Dallas Texans, 1962; Kansas City, 1963–75

Most Fumbles Lost, Season

- 17: Dan Pastorini, Houston, 1973
- 16: Don Meredith, Dallas, 1964
- 15: Paul Christman, Chicago Cardinals, 1946
  Sammy Baugh, Washington, 1947
  Sam Etcheverry, St. Louis, 1961
  Len Dawson, Kansas City, 1964
  Terry Metcalf, St. Louis, 1976

SPORTS LOSERS 135

Most Fumbles Lost, Game

7: Len Dawson, Kansas City vs. San Diego, Nov. 15, 1964
6: Sam Etcheverry, St. Louis vs. New York Giants, Sept. 17, 1961
5: Paul Christman, Chicago Cardinals vs. Green Bay, Nov. 10, 1946
Charlie Connerly, New York Giants vs. San Francisco, Dec. 1, 1957
Jack Kemp, Buffalo vs. Houston, Oct. 29, 1967
Roman Gabriel, Philadelphia vs. Oakland, Nov. 21, 1976

Source: NFL Public Relations Department and Seymour Siwoff, ed., Fran Connors, *Official 1978 National Football League Record Manual*. National Football League, 1978.

Most AFC Championship Games Lost (1960–1979)

Oakland Raiders (7): 1968, 1969, 1970, 1973, 1974, 1975, 1977
San Diego Chargers (4): 1960, 1961, 1964, 1965
Houston Oilers (3): 1967, 1978, 1979
Pittsburgh Steelers (2): 1972, 1976

Most NFC Championship Games Lost (1933–1979)

New York Giants (11): 1933, 1935, 1939, 1941, 1944, 1946, 1958, 1959, 1961, 1962, 1963
Cleveland Browns (7): 1951, 1952, 1953, 1957, 1965, 1968, 1969

136 · THE BOOK OF LOSERS

Los Angeles Rams (7): 1949, 1950, 1955, 1974, 1975, 1976, 1978

Chicago Bears (4): 1934, 1937, 1942, 1956

Dallas Cowboys (4): 1966, 1967, 1972, 1973

Washington Redskins (4): 1936, 1940, 1943, 1945

Source of raw data: *Information Please Almanac: Atlas and Yearbook 1978.* New York: Information Please Pub., Inc., 1977.

Five Greatest Losers in the NFL or AFL Championship Games

1. Washington Redskins, NFL (1940), Margin of Loss: 73 points

Three weeks before the game, the Redskins had defeated the Bears but the score changed dramatically in the championship game. Washington's vaunted defense allowed the Bears to score on their first three possessions, while their ace quarterback corps completed eight passes to the Bears' secondary. To hold the score down, Chicago's star quarterback Sid Luckman sat out the entire second half.

Washington..................	0	0	0	0	0
Chicago.....................	21	7	26	19–73	

2. Detroit Lions, NFL (1954), Margin of Loss: 46 points (10-56)

Coming into the game, the Browns has lost seven consecutive games to the Lions. However, a combination of Detroit ineptitude (6 fumbles and interceptions), and Otto Graham (3 TD passes, 3 rushing TD's) stopped the losing skid.

Detroit.....................	3	7	0	0	10
Cleveland	14	21	14	7–56	

SPORTS LOSERS

3. Cleveland Browns, NFL (1957), Margin of Loss: 45 points (14–59)

Sweet revenge: the Lions returned the favor of three years earlier as they routed the Browns in the championship game. Tobin Rote, filling in for the injured Bobby Lane, riddled the Brown secondary for 218 yards for four touchdown passes.

Cleveland	0	7	7	0–14
Detroit	17	14	14	14–59

4. Boston Patriots, AFL (1963), Margin of Loss: 41 points (10–51)

The Awesome Patriot defense gave up 610 yards total offense to the Chargers. San Diego fullback Keith Lincoln outrushed the entire Patriot team by 73 yards (334–261).

Boston	7	3	0	0–10
San Diego	21	10	7	13–51

5. Chicago Bears, NFL (1956), Margin of Loss: 40 points (7–47)

The Giants ran up 34 points in the first half en route to their passing of the Bears. Frank Gifford caught 4 passes for 131 yards and one touchdown.

Chicago	0	7	0	0– 7
New York	13	21	6	7–47

Closest Losers in NFL or AFL Championship Games

1. Houston Oilers, AFL (1962), Margin of Loss: 3 points in overtime (20–17)

After 17:54 of sudden death, Tommy Brooker's twenty-five-yard field goal gave the Texans the victory, and saved Dallas

138   THE BOOK OF LOSERS

captain Abner Haynes from immortal embarrassment. At the start of the overtime, Haynes won the toss, and gave the wind and the ball to the Oilers.

| Houston | 0 | 0 | 7 | 10 | 0 | 0 – 17 |
| Dallas | 3 | 14 | 0 | 0 | 0 | 3 – 20 |

2. New York Giants, NFL (1958), Margin of Loss: 6 points in overtime (23–17)

The Giants' loss was all the more heartbreaking because the Colts only tied the game with seven seconds left in regulation play. They went on to win on Ameche's one-yard plunge with 8:15 gone in overtime. On the day, Unitas hit 26 of 40 for 349 yards and one TD.

| New York | 3 | 0 | 7 | 7 | 0 – 17 |
| Baltimore | 0 | 14 | 0 | 3 | 6 – 23 |

3. Washington Redskins, NFL (1945), Margin of Loss: 1 point (15–14)

The margin of victory came on a safety in the first quarter. A hurriedly thrown end zone pass by Washington quarterback Sammy Baugh hit the goal post. The game was played on a snow-covered field in 6-degree weather.

| Washington | 0 | 7 | 7 | 0 – 14 |
| Cleveland | 2 | 7 | 6 | 0 – 15 |

Cleveland Browns, NFL (1953), Margin of Loss: 1 point (17–16)

An eighty-yard scoring drive late in the game, capped by a thirty-three-yard TD pass from Bobby Layne, led the Lions to a come-from-behind victory over Cleveland—despite Lou Groza's three field goals and extra point.

| Cleveland | 0 | 3 | 7 | 6 – 16 |
| Detroit | 7 | 3 | 0 | 7 – 17 |

SPORTS LOSERS 139

4. New York Giants, NFL (1933), Margin of Loss: 2 points (23–21)

A bizarre desperation play brought the Giants this loss on fog-shrouded Wrigley field. In the final three minutes, the ball was snapped to Chicago quarterback Carl Brumbaugh, who handed off to fullback Bronco Nagurski, who threw a jump pass to left end Bill Hewitt, who ran fourteen yards and lateraled the ball to right end Bill Karr, who ran nineteen yards for the winning score.

New York	0	7	7	7 – 21
Chicago	3	3	10	7 – 23

Los Angeles Rams, NFL (1950), Margin of Loss: 2 points (30–28)

The game was in doubt until the final twenty seconds, when Lou Groza kicked a twenty-yard winning field goal. Remarkably, both teams amassed 832 yards total offense on a frozen field in falling snow.

Los Angeles	14	0	14	0 – 28
Cleveland	7	6	7	10 – 30

Most Super Bowl Games Lost

1. Minnesota Vikings (4): 1970, 1974, 1975, 1977
2. Dallas Cowboys (4): 1971, 1976, 1978, 1979

Biggest Loser in a Super Bowl Game

Kansas City Chiefs, AFL (1967), Margin of Loss: 25 points (35–10)

The turning point in the first Super Bowl game came when all-pro safety Willy Wood intercepted a Len Dawson pass at the start of the third quarter, and returned it forty yards to the Kansas

THE BOOK OF LOSERS

City five-yard line. This gave Lombardi's Packers momentum as they surged to three second-half touchdowns. Bart Starr was the game's MVP, completing sixteen of twenty-three passes for 250 yards; his favorite receiver in the game, Max McGee, had caught only three passes all season, but caught seven in the game for 138 yards and two touchdowns.

Kansas City	0	10	0	0 – 10
Green Bay	7	7	14	7 – 35

GB–McGee 37 pass from Starr (Chandler kick)
KC–McClinton 7 pass from Dawson (Mercer kick)
GB–Taylor 14 run (Chandler kick)
KC–FG Mercer 31
GB–Pitts 5 run (Chandler kick)
GB–McGee 13 pass from Starr (Chandler kick)
GB–Pitts 1 run (Chandler kick)

Closest Loser in a Super Bowl Game

Dallas Cowboys, NFL (1971), Margin of Loss: 3 points (16–13)

The Colts' only scoring pass came in the second quarter when a Unitas pass bounced through Eddie Hinton's fingertips, off defensive back Mel Renfro's hands, to John Mackey, who galloped forty-five yards to score. In the fourth quarter, Dallas lost the game through interceptions by Rich Volk and Mike Curtis, which set up the Colts' final 10 points. With five seconds left, rookie Jim O'Brien kicked a thirty-two-yard field goal to hand Dallas the loss.

Dallas	3	10	0	0 – 13
Baltimore	0	6	0	10 – 16

Dall–FG Clark 14
Dall–FG Clark 30
Balt–Mackey 75 pass from Unitas (kick blocked)

SPORTS LOSERS

Dall–Thomas 7 pass from Morton (Clark kick)
Balt–Nowatzke 2 run (O'Brien kick)
Balt–FG O'Brien 32

Source of data: *The NFL's Official Encyclopaedic History of Professional Football.* New York: Macmillan, 1976.

BASEBALL LOSERS

1. *Most Games Lost by a Franchise (1900–1979)*

Team	Lost	Won
Philadelphia Phillies (NL)	6742	5540
Boston–Atlanta Braves (NL)	6580	5404
Washington Senators—		
Texas Rangers (AL)	6568	5577
Philadelphia–Kansas City–		
Oakland Athletics (AL)	6397	5723
Cincinnati Reds (NL)	6115	6205
Chicago White Sox (AL)	6038	6109
Chicago Cubs (NL)	5997	6328
Boston Red Sox (AL)	5978	6174
St. Louis Cardinals (NL)	5969	6343
Cleveland Indians (AL)	5895	6276

142 THE BOOK OF LOSERS

2. High Losing Percentage by a Franchise (1900–1979) (at least 200 games played)

Team	Lost	Won	Percentage
St. Louis Browns (AL)	4465	3416	.5665
New York Mets (NL)	1619	1287	.5571
Boston–Atlanta Braves (NL)	6580	5404	.5490
Philadelphia Phillies (NL)	6742	5540	.5489
Washington Senators—			
Texas Rangers (AL)	6568	5577	.5407
Houston Astros (NL)	1544	1362	.5313
Philadelphia–Kansas City–			
Oakland Athletics	6397	5723	.5278
California Angels (AL)	1601	1466	.5220

Primary Source of Raw Data: Frank G. Menke, Pete Palmer: *The Encyclopedia of Sports*, 6th ed. New York: H.S. Barnes & Co., 1978.

3. Twenty Worst Baseball Teams of All Time (all the teams with a losing percentage of more than .701) (1899–present)

Team (Season)	Lost	Won	Losing %
Cleveland (NL) 1899	134	20	.870
Philadelphia (AL) 1916	117	36	.765
Boston (NL) 1935	115	38	.752
New York (NL) 1962	120	40	.750
Washington (AL) 1904	113	38	.749
Philadelphia (AL) 1919	104	36	.743
Pittsburgh (NL) 1952	112	42	.727
Washington (AL) 1909	110	42	.724
Philadelphia (NL) 1942	109	42	.722
Philadelphia (NL) 1941	111	43	.721

SPORTS LOSERS 143

St. Louis (AL) 1939	111	43	.721
Boston (AL) 1932	111	43	.721
Philadelphia (AL) 1915	109	43	.717
Philadelphia (NL) 1928	109	43	.717
Boston (NL) 1911	107	44	.709
Boston (NL) 1909	108	45	.706
St. Louis (AL) 1911	107	45	.704
Philadelphia (NL) 1939	106	45	.702
St. Louis (AL) 1937	108	46	.701
Philadelphia (NL) 1945	108	46	.701

4. Losingest Manager of All Time (loser of most games)

	Losses	Wins	Losing %
Connie Mack: Philadelphia Phillies 1894, 1895, 1896, 1901–1950; includes World Series	4044	3800	.5155

5. Most Consecutive Games Lost

26: Louisville (AA) 1889
24: Cleveland (NL) 1899
23: Philadelphia (NL) 1961
     Pittsburgh (NL) 1890
22: Philadelphia (AA) 1890
20: Boston (AL) 1906
     Philadelphia (AL) 1916
     Philadelphia (AL) 1943
     Louisville (NL) 1894
     Montreal (NL) 1969

144   THE BOOK OF LOSERS

6. Most Games Lost by a Pitcher, Lifetime

308: Cy Young
308: J. F. Galvin (ML)
281: Walter Johnson (AL)
253: J. J. Powell (ML)
251: Eppa Rixey (NL)

7. Most Games Lost by a Pitcher, Season

John Francis Coleman lost 48 games in 1883
V. G. Willis lost 29 games in 1905
J. Townshend lost 27 games in 1904

8. Most Games Lost by a Pitcher, Consecutively

23: Clifton Garfield Curtis (NL) 1910–11
19: Robert Groom (AL) 1909
    John Nabors (AL) 1916
18: Clifton Garfield Curtis (NL) 1910
    Roger L. Craig (NL) 1963

9. Most World Series Lost (to 1979)

Team	Number	Years
Brooklyn/Los Angeles Dodgers	12	1916, 1920, 1941, 1947, 1949, 1952, 1953, 1956, 1966, 1974, 1977. 1978

SPORTS LOSERS   145

New York/San Francisco Giants	10	1911, 1912, 1913, 1917, 1923, 1924, 1936, 1937, 1951, 1962
New York Yankees	10	1921, 1922, 1926, 1942, 1955, 1957, 1960, 1963, 1964, 1976
Chicago Cubs	8	1906, 1910, 1918, 1929, 1932, 1935, 1938, 1945
Detroit Tigers	5	1907, 1908, 1909, 1934, 1940
St. Louis Cardinals	4	1928, 1930, 1943, 1968
Cincinnati Reds	4	1939, 1961, 1970, 1972
Philadelphia Athletics	3	1905, 1914, 1931

(four teams tied with 2)

10. Biggest World Series Losers (all the teams which lost the Series in four straight games)

1907 Detroit Tigers
Led by the immortal Ty Cobb and his .200 batting average in the Series, the Tigers roared to four straight defeats. They actually had a chance to win the first game, but catcher Charley Schmidt dropped a third strike with two out in the bottom of the ninth, and Chicago went on to score two tying runs.

146   *THE BOOK OF LOSERS*

1914 Philadelphia Athletics

This A's team was noted for is "100,000-dollar infield," which proved of little use against the "Miracle Team Boston Braves." The manager of the A's, Connie Mack, was so shocked by his team's performance that he broke up his star-studded squad in the off season—a move of questionable wisdom, since his 1915 team lost 109 and won 43.

1922 New York Yankees

Not to be outdone by Ty Cobb's 1907 Series performance, Babe Ruth whacked out a booming .118 Series average to lead the Yanks to defeat. The Yankees actually tied the second game, when the game was called off on account of darkness with half an hour of daylight left.

1927 Pittsburgh Pirates

Despite the fact that they were facing what many consider the greatest team of all time (the '27 Yankees), the Pirates still had chances to win several games. Nonetheless they found ways to lose, such as in the final game, which they lost by one run when John Miljus wildpitched the winning run home with two out in the ninth.

1928 St. Louis Cardinals

Ruth avenged his poor 1922 showing by hitting .625, including three homes in the final game—despite a lame ankle. Lou Gehrig also had a "good" Series, collecting six hits, four of which were homers.

1932 Chicago Cubs

This was a revenge Series for Yankees manager Joe McCarthy, who had been fired two years earlier by the Cubs. Again in were Ruth and Gehrig, who led the way for the Yanks. Playing in his

SPORTS LOSERS 147

last World Series, Ruth hit two homers, including his incredible blast into the right-field seats after pointing there. Gehrig merely hit three homers, one double, and five singles, and had eight RBIs.

1938 Chicago Cubs

Joe McCarthy beat his former club again. Twenty-two-game winner Bill Lee lost both of his starts against the Yanks, and Dizzy Dean lost a valiant effort in the second game, when Crosetti and DiMaggio hit two-run homers in the eight and ninth innings.

1939 Cincinnati Reds

The Yankees were the culprits again as they wiped out the Reds. The fourth game was indicative of the Reds' plight. Enjoying a 4–2 lead going into the top of the ninth, the Reds committed two costly errors, allowing the Yankees to tie the game. In the tenth they booted two more, and the Yankees scored three more to sweep the Series. Included in the action of the last two innings was catcher Ernie Lombardi's famous "snooze" at home (actually he had been stunned in a collision with King Kong Keller).

1950 Philadelphia Phillies

After winning the pennant in the tenth inning of the last day of the season, Philadelphia's "Whiz Kids" were beaten in four straight by—the Yankees, again. It was no runaway, though; three of the games were decided by one run.

1954 Cleveland Indians

Seven straight years of American League supremacy came to a screeching halt as Cleveland was thrashed by the New York Giants. The Series was marked by Willie Mays's historic catch of

148 THE BOOK OF LOSERS

Vic Rashi's drive to center field in the eighth inning of the opener, which set the tone for the hapless Indians. Dusty Rhodes drove in seven runs in six at bats for the victors, including two game-winning home runs.

1963 New York Yankees
Moose Skowron, Mickey Mantle, Joe Pepitone, Roger Maris—who could stop the mighty Yankees? The answer was simple: Sandy Koufax, Johnny Padres, and Don Drysdale. In four games, the Dodger hurlers limited the Yanks to four runs, in one of the greatest upsets in Series history.

1966 Los Angeles Dodgers
The Dodgers set new records for hitting ineptitude, piling up a grand total of two runs on seventeen hits, and a .142 team batting average. This hitting prowess was climaxed by a streak of thirty-three consecutive scoreless innings. The second game exemplified the Dodgers' misfortunes. Aside from being shut out, they committed six errors, including three on two successive plays in the fifth inning by center-fielder Willy Davis.

1976 New York Yankees
The Big Red Machine was overpowering in the 1976 Series. With such hitters as Johnny Bench (.533 series), George Foster (.429), Dan Driesen (.357), and three others over .300, the Reds were ahead during every inning of the Series except for three innings at the start of the third games.

SPORTS LOSERS 149

15. *Most Heartbreaking World Series Losers (all one-game, one-run losses) (1900–1977)*

1912 New York Giants (three games to four games, final game score 2–3)

Behind three games to one, the Giants rallied to win the next two. The final game went into extra innings with the Giants coming up with one run in the top of the tenth to make the score 2–1. However, in the bottom half of the tenth, outfielder Fred Snodgrass dropped a lazy fly by pinch-hitter Clyde Engle. On the next play, Snodgrass redeemed himself, spearing a deep drive off the bat of Harry Hooper. The next batter walked, sending Engle to second, and bringing Tris Speaker to the bat. Speaker proceeded to lift an easy foul pop which either Chief Meyers or Fred Merkle could have caught, but neither did. Speaker then lined a single to right, scoring Engle, to tie the score. The following batter was walked intentionally to load the bases; whereupon Larry Gardner's sacrifice fly to deep right scored the winning run.

1924 New York Giants (three games to four, final game score 3–4)

The teams traded victories until the deciding seventh game. The Series was marked by the appearance of the old Walter P. Johnson, playing in his first World Series for the Senators, after eighteen years of pitching. The seventh game went twelve innings with the Giants suffering three bad breaks: in the eighth, Harris's grounder took a sudden hop over the head of the Giant third-baseman Lindstrom, allowing the two tying runs to score; in the twelfth, Giant catcher Hank Gowdy dropped a foul fly when he accidentally stepped on his mask; and on the final play of the Series, Earl McNeely's grounder took a weird bounce over

150   *THE BOOK OF LOSERS*

Lindstrom's head to drive in the winning run. The winning pitcher was Walter Johnson.

1926 New York Yankees (three games to four, final game score 2–3)

The Yankees were led by Babe Ruth, who blasted four homers, three of them in the fourth game, but they were ultimately defeated by the thirty-nine-year-old Grover Cleveland Alexander who won the second and sixth games. Nonetheless, the Yankees seemed on the verge of pulling the Series out in the final game. In the bottom of the seventh, they scored one run and had the bases loaded with Tony Lazzeri coming to bat. At this point, Rogers Hornsby, the St. Louis manager, decided to bring in Alexander from the bullpen—even though he had pitched the previous day. Alexander proceeded to strike out Lazzeri to end the inning, and pitch hitless ball during the eighth and ninth to insure the Yankees' defeat.

1940 Detroit Tigers (three games to four, final game score 1–2)

The Tigers were led by Bobo Newsome, whose victory in the first game was marred by the heart attack and death to his father a few hours after the game. Dedicating the fifth game of his father, Newsome shut out Cincinnati 8–0. However, in the Series final, inept fielding allowed Cincinnati to score two runs in the bottom of the seventh to defeat Newsome and the Tigers 2–1.

1946 Boston Red Sox (three games to four, final game score 3–4)

The Red Sox were led by Ted Williams's blazing .200 batting average in the Series—a result of trying to pull the ball against Lou Boudreau's overshifted defense. The underdog St. Louis team was led by the ever-hustling Enos Slaughter. With two out

SPORTS LOSERS 151

and the score tied in the eighth inning of the final game, Slaughter scored all the way from first on Harry Walker's single over the shortstop's head to win the game for the Cards.

1960 New York Yankees (three games to four, final game score 9–10)

The Yankees' loss was made remarkable by the fact that the Bronx bombers set Series records for highest team batting average (.338), most runs (55), most hits (91), most total bases (142), and most RBI (54). Going into the final game, the Yankees had won their three games by a combined score of 38–3. In the seventh game, Pittsburgh scored four runs off of Turley and Stafford in the first two innings. In the fifth and sixth innings the Yankees roared back on the strength of homers by Moose Skowron and Yogi Berra to a 5–4 lead, which they padded to 7–4 in the top of the eighth. However, with their backs to the wall, the Pirates erupted for five runs in the bottom of the inning capped by Hal Smith's tremendous three-run blast to left. But the Yankees didn't quit, scoring two more in the top of the ninth to tie the game at 9–9. Then, in the bottom of the ninth, the Pirates' lead-off batter Bill Mazeroski clobbered Ralph Terry's second pitch over Berra's head and the left field wall to give the Pirates a 10–9 win.

1962 San Francisco Giants (three games to four, final game score 0–1)

The Giants' pitching staff did a masterful job of holding the Yankees' vaunted hitters to a combined Series batting average of .199. Nonetheless, the Yankees were not to be denied, and they rallied to win the seventh game behind the four-hit pitching of Ralph Terry. The Yankees themselves only managed seven hits off Jack Sanford, but managed to score one run in the fifth. During the inning, Skowron and Clete Boyer singled, bringing

152 THE BOOK OF LOSERS

up the pitcher. Sanford momentarily lost control and walked
Terry to load the bases. Skowron then scored when Tony Kubek
grounded into a double play.

1971 Baltimore Orioles (three games to four, final game score 1–2)

The Orioles got off to a quick start, winning the first two
games, in Baltimore. Then the Pirates rallied to take the next two
games, and the teams swapped victories in games five and six. In
the dramatic seventh game, Roberto Clemente, who hit .414 for
the Series, homered in the fourth inning to give the Pirates a 1–0
lead. In the top of the eighth the Pirates added another run when
Willie Stargell scored on a double by José Pagan. The Orioles
attempted to mount an attack in the bottom of the eighth.
However, with men on second and third and only one out, they
could get only one run across.

1972 Cincinnati Reds (three games to four, final game score 2–3)

This was the closest World Series ever played, with every game
but the sixth being decided by one run. The final game featured
pitching from four different A's pitchers (Odom, Hunter,
Holtzman, Fingers) and five different Red hurlers (Billingham,
Borbon, Carroll, Grimsley, and Hall). The A's won the game by
scoring two runs in the top of the sixth inning, on RBI doubles
by Gene Tenace and Sal Bando. Catfish Hunter got credit for the
victory.

1975 Boston Red Sox (three games to four, final game score 3–4)

The Series will probably be remembered most for its dramatic
sixth game, which the Red Sox won 7–6. The game featured
many dramatic fielding plays, such as George Foster's game-
saving catch and throw to the plate for the Reds in the ninth, and

SPORTS LOSERS 153

Dwight Evan's incredible catch of Joe Morgan's line drive to right in the eleventh for the Red Sox. The game was won in equally dramatic fashion when Carlton Fisk homered off the left field foul pole in the bottom of the twelfth. The final game came somewhat as an anticlimax, and was won in the top of the ninth on Joe Morgan's bloop RBI single.

Primary source of raw data for Baseball section: Hy Turkin, S. C. Thompson, and Pete Palmer, *The Official Encyclopedia of Baseball* (9th ed.). Garden City: Dolphin, 1977.

BASKETBALL—COLLEGE LOSERS

1. Most Losses by an NAIA Small College Team

West Virginia Wesleyan (1968): Lost 24, Won 0.

2. Most Consecutive Losses by an NAIA Small College Team

West Virginia Wesleyan, 29

3. Biggest Loss by an NAIA Small College Team

Shimer, Illinois, by 108 points. On November 28, 1967, Shimer lost to Rockford, Illinois, by a score of 154–46.

4. Most Games Lost by a College Basketball Team (1938–1972)

Team	Lost	Won
Virginia Military Institute	524	182
Idaho	522	426
University of Denver	490	377
University of Georgia	483	353
Texas Christian	482	361
Clemson	480	315
Montana	477	416
Brown	476	329
Harvard	473	324
Texas A&M	466	365

5. Highest Losing Percentages by College Basketball Teams (1938–1972)

Team	Lost	Won	Losing %
Virginia Military Institute	524	182	.742
New Hampshire	434	215	.669
Lehigh	443	241	.648
Clemson	480	315	.604
Harvard	473	324	.593
Brown	476	329	.591
The Citadel	429	299	.589
North Texas State	456	328	.582
University of Mississippi	460	332	.581
University of Georgia	483	353	.578

SPORTS LOSERS 155

6. 26 Worst College Basketball Teams (at least fourteen games played) (1938–1972)

Team	Year	Lost	Won
Virginia Military	1944	14	0
Baylor	1945	14	0
Virginia Military	1971	25	1
The Citadel	1955	22	1
New Hampshire	1968	22	1
Rice	1966	22	1
Tulane	1964	22	1
Maryland	1941	21	1
Texas Christian	1947	21	1
The Citadel	1954	18	1
West Texas State	1967	18	1
The Citadel	1949	17	1
Louisville	1939	16	1
Massachusetts	1940	14	1
University of Denver	1969	24	2
Nevada–Reno	1972	24	2
Pepperdine	1956	24	2
San José State	1971	24	2
Dartmouth	1964	23	2
Georgia Tech	1954	22	2
North Texas State	1961	22	2
Rice	1965	22	2
Syracuse	1962	22	2
Texas A&M	1954	20	2
Northwestern	1956	20	2
Western Michigan	1959	20	2

156   *THE BOOK OF LOSERS*

7. *Most NIT Championship Game Losses (to 1973)*

Dayton (5): 1951, 1952, 1955, 1956, 1958
New York University (3): 1945, 1948, 1966
St. John's (3): 1953, 1962, 1970

BASKETBALL—PROFESSIONAL LOSERS

1. *Biggest Loser in One Game*

On March 19, 1972, the Golden State Warriors lost to the Los Angeles Lakers by a margin of 63 points (99–162).

2. *Nine Franchises with the Highest Losing Percentage Since Their Inception (at least seven seasons)*

Team (years)	Lost	Won	Losing %
Buffalo Braves (1970–78)/			
San Diego Clippers (1979)	436	302	.590
Cleveland Cavaliers			
(1970–79)	434	304	.588
Houston Rockets (1967–79)	561	423	.570
Portland Trail Blazers			
(1970–79)	416	322	.563
Fort Wayne/Detroit Pistons			
(1948–79)	1312	1070	.550
Phoenix Suns (1968–79)	475	427	.526

Seattle Supersonics (1967–79)	522	482	.519
St. Louis/Atlanta Hawks (1949–79)	1195	1125	.515
Cincinnati Royals/Kansas City Kings (1948–79)	1208	1172	.507

3. Five Franchises That Have Lost the Most Games

Team	Lost	Won
Fort Wayne/Detroit Pistons	1312	1070
New York Knicks	1242	1247
San Francisco/Golden State Warriors	1224	1264
Cincinnati Royals/Kansas City Kings	1208	1172
St. Louis/Atlanta Hawks	1195	1125

4. All-Time Worst Teams (Highest Losing Percentage) (1947–1979)

Team (year)	Lost	Won	Losing %
Providence Steam Rollers (1947–48)	42	6	.875
Philadelphia (1973)	73	9	.890
San Francisco (1952–53)	57	12	.826
Cleveland (1970–71)	67	15	.817
Houston (1967–78)	67	15	.817
Denver (1949–50)	51	11	.822
Phoenix (1968–69)	66	16	.804
San Francisco (1964–65)	63	17	.787
Portland (1971–72)	64	18	.777
Baltimore (1953–54)	56	16	.777

158   *THE BOOK OF LOSERS*

5. *Most Consecutive Games Lost*

Philadelphia (20): January 9—February 11, 1973
San Francisco (17): December 20, 1964—January 26, 1965
San Diego (later Houston) (17): January 17—February 18, 1968

6. *Most NBA Championships Lost (to 1979)*

Lost Angeles Lakers (8): 1973, 1970, 1969, 1968, 1966, 1965, 1963, 1962
New York Knicks (4): 1972, 1953, 1952, 1951
Atlanta/St. Louis Hawks (3): 1961, 1960, 1957

7. *Biggest NBA Championship Series Losers (all the teams that lost the Series in four straight games) (to 1979)*

Minneapolis Lakers (1959)
Baltimore Bullets (1971)
Washington Bullets (1975)

Primary sources of raw data for Basketball section:

Zander Hollander, ed., *The Modern Encyclopedia of Basketball*. New York: Four Winds Press, 1973.

Frank G. Menke, *The Encyclopedia of Sports*. New York: A.S. Barnes, 1969.

YACHTING LOSERS

1. Most Losses in the America's Cup Races

England (11)

Year	Ship	Owner
1851	Avrora	T. Le Merdiant
1870	Cambria	James Asbury
1871	Livonia	James Asbury
1885	Genesta	Richard Sutton
1886	Galatea	William Henn
1893	Valkyrie II	Lord Dunraven
1895	Valkyrie III	Lord Dunraven
1934	Endeavor	T.O.M. Sopwith
1937	Endeavor II	T.O.M. Sopwith
1958	Sceptre	Hugh Goodson
1964	Sovereign	J. Bowden

2. Most Consecutive Losses by an Owner in America's Cup Races

Ireland (5): Thomas Lipton

1899	Shamrock I
1901	Shamrock II
1903	Shamrock III
1920	Shamrock IV
1930	Shamrock V

Source of raw data: *Information Please Almanac: Atlas and Yearbook 1978.* New York: Information Please Pub., Inc. 1977.

160   *THE BOOK OF LOSERS*

HEAVYWEIGHT BOXING LOSERS

Fighters Who Lost the Most Heavyweight Championship Fights (through 6/1/80)

Fights Lost	Fighter	Dates of Losing Bouts
6	Joe Walcott	12/5/47, 6/25/48, 6/22/49, 3/7/51, 9/23/52, 5/15/53
4	Floyd Patterson	6/26/59, 10/25/61, 7/22/63, 12/11/65
4	Ezzard Charles	7/18/51, 6/5/52, 6/17/54, 10/17/54
3	James J. Corbett	3/17/1897, 5/11/1900, 8/14/1903
3	Bill Squires	7/14/1907, 6/13/1908, 8/24/1908

Source of raw data: *The World Almanac, 1977.* New York: Newspaper Enterprise Assn., 1977.

I am happy that you have survived until this point. I would appreciate your comments about the book.

1. Please tell me what you enjoyed most and least about the book.

2. If you have happened upon any errors or omissions, let me know.

3. If you have any suggestions about what you'd like to see in the next edition, send me your ideas.

You can mail your letter or card to this address:

George Rooks, *The Book of Losers*
c/o St. Martin's Press
175 Fifth Ave.
New York, N.Y., 10010